T0270624

WOMEN ROCK!

Portraits in Popular Music

whitestar

"I didn't want to be the girl singer in the band. I wanted to be the band. I wanted to sing the songs that the guys would sing....What I was looking for was to be Mick Jagger or Robert Plant."

—Pat Benatar

WOMEN ROCK!

Portraits in Popular Music

text by **Philip Auslander**

Contents

Introduction

Chrissie Hynde, leader of the rock band the Pretenders, once said in a radio interview that she does not want to be labeled a "woman in rock" but wants to be seen as a rock musician who is a woman and whose music should be appreciated for its inherent qualities, not for the gender of the person who made it. This is an entirely understandable position, shared by many female-identified musicians, including others represented in this book. But with all due respect to Hynde, it is a social and cultural fact that music is gendered. In the United States at present, around 80 percent of professional musicians are men, making music a heavily male-dominated pursuit and depriving young women who aspire to be musicians of female role models. Women are better represented if one looks at popular music specifically, but the difference is not dramatic: about 30 percent of popular music artists are women. Breaking the figures down further by genre, women musicians in pop—widely considered to be a female-dominated genre—constitute 32 percent. The numbers for other genres are significantly smaller. The next highest is dance music at 21.5 percent; in no other genre do women reach a threshold of 20 percent. Considering that the world's population is just under 50 percent female, women are seriously under-represented as musicians.

> "It seems to me that being a pop star is almost like being in a type of prison. You have to be a good girl."
>
> —Sinéad O'Connor

While it is true that any person, female or male, can participate in any kind of music as a fan or performer, it is equally true that the male dominance of music derives from long-established and deeply ingrained social assumptions that constrain women far more than men. Madonna once credited David Bowie as her role model, saying, "He made me think there were no rules." She went on to say, however, "But I was wrong. There are no rules—if you're a boy. There are rules if you're a girl." As far back as 1528, Baldassare Castiglione, the Italian author of *The Book of the Courtier*, a guide to courtly etiquette, proposed that a woman "should choose instruments suited to her purpose. Imagine what an ungainly sight it would be to have a woman playing drums, fifes, trumpets, or other instruments of the sort; this is simply because their stridency buries and destroys the sweet gentleness that embellishes everything a woman does."

The idea of gender-appropriate musical instruments, according to which higher-pitched, supposedly more delicate instruments are considered feminine and lower-pitched, more forceful instruments are thought of as masculine, persists well into the twenty-first century. One study published in 2008 found that when selecting instruments in an educational setting, "girls predominated in harp, flute, voice, fife/piccolo, clarinet, oboe, and violin, and boys in electric guitar, bass guitar, tuba, kit drums, tabla, and trombone." When asked about their preferred instruments, drums are the second most popular choice for girls, but only 20 percent of girls become drummers. How a person gravitates toward one instrument as opposed to another is complex, but from an early age, girls are steered by parents, teachers,

and themselves toward some instruments and away from others. The acoustic guitar is considered "lady-like"; the electric guitar is not. In the eighteenth and nineteenth centuries, the guitar was not perceived as a professional musical instrument but as a domestic one highly suitable for women, an association it has retained. The electric guitar, however, is not seen in this way. Because of its association with rock and jazz, it is perceived as a man's instrument, an idea that is reinforced by other cultural representations. A study of advertisements that appeared from the 1940s through the 1960s in a popular magazine aimed at a female readership observes that "girls were pictured...standing near guitars, and watching boys playing guitars, but rarely was a girl shown holding or playing a guitar." The pressure to play acoustic rather than electric guitar—and to play folk music rather than rock—so irritated the young Joan Jett that she refused to touch an acoustic guitar until she chose to make an "unplugged" album in 2020.

One result of the social link between gender roles and musical roles is that some women who are interested in playing electric guitar turn instead toward more traditionally "feminine" musical functions, such as singing. In rock music, there is an unfortunate distinction between instrumentalists and singers. To be a truly authentic rocker, ideally one must play electric guitar. It is entirely acceptable for a woman to front a rock band as a singer, but the role of "chick singer" to which women are often confined is a stereotyped and limited one. Suzi Quatro, for one, has long emphasized that if women want to break down gender norms in rock, they must do so as instrumentalists, not just singers. Jett, Hynde, and others have suggested similar views. On the one hand, this acknowledges the strength of the connection between the electric guitar and rock authenticity and encourages women to participate in the genre on its own terms. On the other hand, it reinforces the denigration of singers in rock, tacitly dismissing the undeniable importance and contributions of women who perform primarily or exclusively as singers. The list of singers included in this book alone is a roster of great musicians from numerous rock subgenres that includes Pat Benatar, Doro, Nico, Nina Hagen, Skin, Kathleen Hanna, Debbie Harry, Janis Joplin, Annie Lennox, Stevie Nicks, Sinéad O'Connor, Linda Ronstadt, Siouxsie Sioux, Patti Smith, Grace Slick, and Ann Wilson. There are many other genres of popular music in which singers are revered and no premium is placed on being an instrumentalist. No one expects Beyoncé, Cher, Madonna, Aretha Franklin, Diana Ross, or Tina Turner to strap on an electric guitar, though Franklin was a skilled pianist who performed jazz and blues before turning to soul music, and Madonna began her career as a guitarist and drummer in bands. It is observable that some singers outside of rock, including Dolly Parton, Taylor Swift, Madonna, and Shakira, sometimes play guitar on stage to round out their images as musicians.

With respect to the role of rock instrumentalist, women are confronted with a "damned if they do, damned if they don't" scenario. In terms of rock ideology, a woman who does not play an appropriate instrument is not respected as a musician. On the other hand, the women who challenge the norm by becoming electric guitarists frequently are not taken seriously in that capacity and are subjected to taunts and dismissal. Nancy Wilson of Heart, a highly accomplished guitarist, recalls being asked whether she could really play her guitar or if it was just a prop. A reluctance to subject oneself to such belittling may explain why such greatly skilled musicians as Wilson, Bonnie Raitt, and Melissa Etheridge all hesitated to play lead guitar in their respective bands, initially deferring to male guitarists and taking over the lead position only after they were established artists.

As the journalist and music critic David Segal points out, the scarcity of women guitarists becomes a self-fulfilling prophecy: "Girls don't see women play the guitar, which stigmatizes the instrument a bit, further discouraging girls from taking up guitar, and so on." Joan Jett also notes the way social strictures are continually reiterated: "There's a thing on a loop about what girls can achieve. When they come up, you've got to challenge those assumptions at every turn." In addition to Jett and everyone else in this book, all of whom show that conventions and limitations can be overcome by challenging them, others have attacked the problem from different angles. Organizations offer summer camps specifically for girls who want to learn to play rock music, for instance. In 2000, musician Tish Ciravolo founded Daisy Rock Guitars, a company that manufactures and markets the instruments specifically for girls and women, in colors and designs meant to appeal to a feminine sensibility and offering a signature model associated with the all-woman rock band the Bangles. One seldom-discussed dimension of the problem is that traditional guitars are not well-suited to the female body. As the guitar became associated with masculinity, it also became larger and heavier, making it more difficult for at least some women to play. Welsh musician Cate Le Bon points out that "guitars were inspired by female bodies" and goes on to ask, "Why are they uncomfortable for women to play?" Daisy Guitars are designed to be compatible with the bodies of girls and women, and in 2016, the rock musician St. Vincent (Annie Clark) worked with Ernie Ball Music Man to develop a guitar she designed that, in her words, allows "room for a breast. Or two."

More than two-thirds of the artists included in *Rock Like a Woman!* can be considered rock musicians, broadly defined. The history of rock music is inextricable from the countercultural context in which it developed in the second half of the 1960s. As historian Alice Echols points out, the gender ideology of the hippie movement was every bit as male-centered as that of the bourgeois society the hippies claimed to repudiate. Women were expected to remain in the domestic sphere and be subordinate to men, making the counterculture inhospitable to "ambitious, creative women." Tracy Nelson, a blues-rock musician who moved to San Francisco, the epicenter of the counterculture, in 1966 remarks, "I don't know how many musicians [told] me, 'Why do you want to do this? This is no place for women. This is no business for a woman.' You know, 'Why not just stay home, find a man.'" This obviously does not mean there were no "women in rock" in the 1960s—actually, there were more than is usually acknowledged, of whom Nelson is one. However, because rock music was perceived as a male-dominated genre from its very beginnings, female musicians did not have the same opportunities or gain the same recognition as their male counterparts. For example, the Ace of Cups, the only all-female rock band on the San Francisco hippie scene, shared bills with many of the biggest names in rock at the time yet never had the opportunity to make the records that might have gained them a bigger audience. After disbanding in 1972, the group reformed in 2016 and are now enjoying in their seventies the career they possibly could have had then.

Not only are popular music genres male-dominated in a statistical sense, but the history of popular music is also usually written in a way that suggests that while women may participate, men are the creative forces behind and originators of musical genres. The story of soul music is frequently told in this way, its origins attributed to Ray Charles, Sam Cooke, and others. Aretha Franklin, the Queen of Soul who defined the genre for the 1960s, is often mentioned as an important participant, perhaps a key figure, but not as an innovator. Women's contributions to the development of rock and roll are similarly downplayed or simply excluded from historical accounts. Part of Segal's explanation for why there are so few female rock guitarists is that "women basically sat out, or were sidelined during, the first 20 years of the development of the rock guitar," and by the time they came on the scene, all the possibilities of how rock could be played on the guitar had been explored and exhausted. But there is another way of telling the story in which female guitarists did not sit out the origins of rock guitar but created it. Sister Rosetta Tharpe, a guitarist and singer with roots in gospel who worked with swing bands in the 1940s and as a solo act through the 1960s, developed a way of mingling jazz, blues, and gospel in her playing to create a style that sounds very much like Chuck Berry's, only she was playing this way more than ten years earlier than Berry. Whereas Berry is frequently described as an "inventor" and "pioneer" of rock and roll, Tharpe, arguably the creator of a crucial aspect of the genre, is relegated to the status of "godmother" or "forebear" even by sympathetic commentators. She was inducted posthumously into the Rock and Roll Hall of Fame as an "early influence" rather than as a rock and roll artist in her own right. Peggy Jones, known as "Lady Bo" because of her association with the first-generation rock and roller Bo Diddley, is another overlooked figure who was there at the creation of rock and roll, credited with being the first female lead guitarist in the genre. Diddley was an established artist when Jones joined his band in 1957, but she contributed materially to the development of the famous Bo Diddley sound in the studio and onstage. She and Diddley traded off lead

> "I never found it harder because I'm a woman. If anything I've been treated better. Guys will carry my guitars and stuff—who's going to say no? Guys always tune my guitars, too."
>
> —Chrissie Hynde

and rhythm guitar parts to the degree that they have been described as sounding like a single player. Because the idea of a female guitarist in rock and roll was so incongruous in the 1950s, Jones was subjected to the same skepticism visited on female rock guitarists a quarter of a century later. It was rumored that she did not really play at concerts, that her parts were played back from recordings. "Aztec" (1960), an instrumental Jones wrote and on which she plays multiple guitar parts in a style related to surf music, was a European hit mistakenly credited to Diddley.

The failure to take adequate account of women's musical contributions continued into the rock era. Tracy McMullen, in her book *Haunthenticity: Musical Replay and the Fear of the Real*, makes a trenchant case that although Janis Joplin is one of the few women who is regularly acknowledged in accounts of rock in the 1960s, she has been erased from the music's history as the originator of the vocal styles associated with hard rock and heavy metal. Robert Plant of Led Zeppelin is considered a key figure in this development. In early discussions of the group, he was sometimes described as "the male Janis Joplin," not just for his singing but also for his stage mannerisms, movements, and gestures. Over time, however, Joplin has disappeared from the story so that Plant becomes the progenitor of this vocal style rather than someone who was influenced by its progenitor. Many assumptions about the gendering of rock music would be undermined by acknowledging Tharpe's and Jones's contributions to the development of rock and roll guitar style, let alone by acknowledging that a woman is the originator of the kind of singing associated with rock's most macho subgenres.

The artists included in this book come from many genres of music in addition to rock, including pop, folk, soul, R&B, country, singer-songwriter, dance, heavy metal, and Latin music. Not all these contexts have been as resistant to women's participation as rock. The first and second waves of the folk music revival, for instance, were driven by a democratic, egalitarian ideology that created space for both men and women. While many of the movement's architects were men, like Pete Seeger, singer Sis Cunningham, the founding editor of the magazine *Broadside*, a key organ of the Greenwich Village folk revival that published songs and recorded artists, was a crucial part of the scene's infrastructure. In the 1940s, Cunningham had also been part of the Almanac Singers, a highly political musical collective that was formative to the first wave of the folk revival. The first stars of second wave folk in the early 1960s were women like Joan Baez, Judy Collins, and Mary Travers of Peter, Paul and Mary. These musicians and others asserted women's ability to make their own music without being beholden to men and became role models for subsequent cohorts of female musicians. The folk community also served as a starting point for other women across several generations, including Joni Mitchell, Janis Joplin, Bonnie Raitt, Nancy Wilson, Linda Ronstadt, and Tracy Chapman.

The difference between the context that surrounded folk music in the early 1960s and the one that surrounded rock music in the later 1960s speaks to the importance of music scenes. A scene is understood to be a musical community usually anchored in a specific place, time, and genre. In terms of gender, some scenes have been more welcoming of women as musicians than others. The Los Angeles Laurel Canyon scene in the early 1970s, which was crucial to the evolution of the singer-songwriter genre, was a home to many important women musicians, including Cass Elliot of the Mamas and the Papas, Joni Mitchell, Linda Ronstadt, Carole King, and Bonnie Raitt. The punk rock scene, in both its original form in the mid-1970s associated with New York and London, and its revived form on the West Coast of the United States in the 1990s, was a scene on which women found a positive reception. Many of the figures profiled here emerged from the Laurel Canyon scene and from punk, post-punk, and new wave scenes in the US, the UK, and Europe. The latter include Björk, Nina Hagen, Debbie Harry, Courtney Love, Siouxsie Sioux, and Patti Smith. Chrissie Hynde, an American living in London at the time of punk, took inspiration from it without feeling a part of it. By contrast, the grunge scene of the 1990s was perceived as being extremely hostile toward women in that women musicians were not respected by their male colleagues, and female musicians and fans alike were subjected to abusive treatment at performances. The musical dimension of riot grrrl, a radical feminist cultural and political movement, addressed this through aggressive punk music that exposed sexual violence and critiqued the culture that gives rise to it. Bikini Kill frontwoman Kathleen Hanna's famous rallying cry "Girls to the front!" literally demanded the creation of a safe space for women—including those onstage—in concert settings, but it also articulated the need to foreground women's experience in cultural expression and rock.

11 Tina Turner onstage during one of her tireless rock performances.

Riot grrrl was not the first popular music scene to focus on women or to suggest that women need their own musical space. The women's music (sometimes stylized as "womyn's music") movement began in the early 1970s alongside the evolution of second wave feminism and the gay rights movement. Whereas riot grrrl operated in the same contexts as male punk and grunge musicians, the women's music movement was largely separatist and lesbian in orientation. The music was made by women, about women, and intended for an audience of women; festivals devoted to it often excluded men. The most established of these, the Michigan Womyn's Music Festival, ran from 1974 through 2015. Lilith Fair, a traveling music festival organized by Canadian musician Sarah McLachlan that toured during the summers of 1997 to 1999, carried on the idea of a festival devoted to female musicians in a more mainstream context. Olivia Records, founded in 1974 by a collective of ten women and active through 1988, was the main outlet for the women's music movement, featuring artists such as Meg Christian, Cris Williamson, and Linda Tillery, who previously had been the lead singer for the Loading Zone, a band on the San Francisco psychedelic rock scene in the late 1960s. Much of the music made under this banner was acoustic and folk oriented. In 1974, Holly Near, a major figure in the women's music movement, dedicated an album to Ronnie Gilbert, a heroine of hers who had been a member of the Weavers, the most popular first-wave folk group of the 1940s and 1950s. After discovering that Gilbert was still alive, Near toured and recorded with her in 1983.

Apart from organized movements like women's music and riot grrrl and businesses designed to further the cause of women in music, such as Daisy Guitars, female musicians have found myriad ways of supporting one another. Although Christine McVie and Stevie Nicks joined Fleetwood Mac at very different moments in the group's history, they became friends and joined forces to create a united front against efforts by the music industry and the male members of the band to treat them unequally. Natalie Merchant of 10,000 Maniacs asked Tracy Chapman to serve as the band's opening act, then invited her back onstage to sing with her and extoll her talent. The established Latin artist Gloria Estefan played a significant role in helping Shakira cross over from the Spanish-language market into the English-language market. Beyoncé conspicuously employs female instrumentalists in her band and showcases them in solo spots rather than just using them as her backup. In an industry in which fewer than 3 percent of record producers are women, artists have stepped into the gap by producing for each other. Joan Jett has produced records for Bikini Kill and Wanda Jackson. Kim Gordon of Sonic Youth produced *Pretty on the Inside*, the debut album by Courtney Love's band Hole. Many of the artists included here have produced their own recordings at one point or another. Women who have made inroads into the industry by starting their own record labels include Madonna, Melissa Etheridge, Kate Bush, the Bangles, Katy Perry, and Ani DiFranco, who has never recorded for a label other than her own. In the words of Eurythmics' feminist anthem, sung by Annie Lennox and Aretha Franklin, "Sisters are doin' it for themselves!"

Sinéad O'Connor has said, "Whether we like it or not, us females in the industry are role models." Though she was referring primarily to the impact musicians have as public figures, she said this in 2013 in an open letter to the singer Miley Cyrus in which she attempts to mentor the younger woman, who she felt was allowing herself to be objectified in her performances and videos. The absence of role models for aspiring female musicians is a function of women's minority status in popular music that has spurred much discussion. Suzi Quatro, for example, claims that since there were no suitable women role models for her as a would-be female rocker in the 1960s, she took inspiration from male performers, particularly Elvis Presley. Over time, more female musical role models have become available as women of one generation inspire those of subsequent ones. After helping to define the identity of woman rocker, Quatro became a role model to younger women aspiring to that role, notably Joan Jett. Dolly Parton has been an avowed role model for many younger women in country music, including Taylor Swift, Carrie Underwood, and Miley Cyrus. In her book *Frock Rock: Women Performing Popular Music*, sociologist and musician Mavis Bayton reports that the older women musicians she interviewed cited only two role models: Quatro and Hynde. Younger women who benefited from women's greater participation in music that began with punk listed around twenty figures they consider role models, including many represented in *Rock Like a Woman!* Bayton published her book in 1998; the list of role models available to young female musicians has surely increased enormously since.

Music is not just heard—it is also seen. The visual dimensions of musical performance are an essential part of the experience of music. However, women confront specific issues around visibility as performers because of the sexual objectification of women that is rampant in male-dominated societies. One impetus for the creation of the women-only or women-to-the-front performance spaces discussed earlier was the offensive and objectifying behaviors to which women musicians are frequently subjected. Male audience members regularly heckle female performers, demanding that they undress and worse. According to Bayton in *Frock Rock: Women Performing Popular Music*, this creates a situation in which female musicians agonize over their appearance, over how feminine or masculine they can afford to appear, and often feel that they must present themselves in ways other than they would like to conform to genre expectations or preemptively blunt prospective abuse from the audience.

In 1981, the cable television channel MTV (Music Television) ushered in the age of the music video, in which short films became an indispensable means of marketing music, particularly for new artists, making musicians more aware than ever of their images and the visual dimensions of their performances. This proved to be a double-edged sword for women. Some, like Pat Benatar, Madonna, and Annie Lennox, built videos around striking personae that helped make them stars and fashion icons, a tactic also employed successfully by artists of later generations, such as Beyoncé and Lady Gaga. Others, however, including sisters Ann and Nancy Wilson of Heart, feared that music videos placed too much emphasis on the visual and thus reinforced society's reduction of women to their appearances.

Both Siouxsie Sioux and Alanis Morissette use the word "ornamental" when describing the roles women musicians are expected to play. As with the choice of musical instruments already mentioned, the expectations imposed on female musician are social in origin. Morissette observes, "I'd always been taught from a very young age as a female that there was more importance in the ornamental part of myself rather than the instrumental part." One response to this on the part of musicians like Sinéad O'Connor, Billie Eilish, and others is to conspicuously refuse to cooperate in their own objectification by designing what could be called anti-ornamental personae that fly in the face of conventional femininity. When told by a record executive to grow out her hair to appear more feminine, Sinéad O'Connor shaved her head instead. Both she and Eilish wear baggy, non-revealing clothing. Eilish has critiqued her own objectification and the media's prurient interest in her body in her songs, videos, and performances. Exercising another strategy, both Debbie Harry and Dolly Parton embody—admittedly very different—versions of hyper-femininity that critique the stereotypes from which they're drawn by exaggerating them.

Circling back to where I started, with Chrissie Hynde's desire to be seen as a musician who is a woman rather than a woman musician, I sympathize with her position and envision a world in which musical achievement can be appreciated for itself without consideration of gender. But I don't think we live in that world yet. The situation

record producers are women, as are less than 9 percent of recording engineers and just over 7 percent of studio musicians. Gender should not matter to music, but to act as if it does not would be to ignore these obvious inequities.

This is not just a matter of numbers. It is also a question of the cultures around popular music genres and how receptive they are to women's participation. In 2021, rock musician Phoebe Bridgers attempted to destroy her guitar by smashing it into her amplifier at the end of a performance on the US television program *Saturday Night Live*. She was not the first rock musician to smash a guitar,

of female popular musicians certainly has improved over time, but how much? Women are still seriously under-represented in the music industry, whether one looks at the ranks of artists or those of gatekeepers such as record label executives and radio programmers. The percentage of radio disc jockeys who are female is similar to the percentage of women in popular music, around 36 percent. Only 10 percent of the songs played on country music stations are by women, and country radio programmers advise stations not to play two songs by women in a row, ostensibly because there are so few they need to be spread out, or to maintain male hegemony in the genre by not playing them at all. As mentioned earlier, less than 3 percent of

an action that has a long history in the genre dating back to Pete Townshend's smashing of guitars with the Who and Jimi Hendrix's destruction of guitars in the 1960s. But rather than seeing Bridgers as a young musician aligning herself with that history by employing an established trope of rock performance, much of the immediate response to her action implied that she did not have the right to smash a guitar and thus claim a place in the genre. Different reasons why she did not have this right were put forward, but as Marianne Eloise wrote in *Guitar World*, the criticism was fundamentally misogynist: "What they're thinly veiling is the fact that they're just pissed off because she's a woman."

"What Suzi Quatro did for me was make me realize that girls could be successful playing rock'n'roll. I realized that if I wanted to do that, there were probably other girls like me who probably wanted to do it, too."

—Joan Jett

A word about the profiles gathered in this book. Short biographies, career overviews, and discographies for the figures discussed here are readily available online and elsewhere. Some have been the subjects of full-scale biographies or have authored autobiographies or memoirs. I have not attempted here to paint complete portraits but rather to sketch some salient points about these women as musicians, performers, artists, and people with something to say.

The women of popular music deserve to be celebrated, and this is what *Rock Like a Woman!* aims to do. I hope these portraits will whet your appetite to find out more about these musicians and, above all, to listen to their music. At the end of the day, it is about the music.

14 left Aretha Franklin singing at NBC Studios in 1976.

14 right Joan Baez performs at her induction ceremony in the Rock and Roll Hall of Fame in 2017.

15 left Patti Smith during one of her live iconic performances in 2005.

15 right Billie Eilish performs at a music festival in Austin, Texas, in 2021.

THE VOICE OF
HER GENERATION

JOAN BAEZ

< With her acoustic
guitar her only
accompaniment, Joan
Baez performs at the
Ravinia Festival in 1968.

As a teenage performer in the 1950s, Joan Baez sang the rock and roll songs of the time. She credits seeing Pete Seeger in concert with inspiring her to gravitate toward folk music, concluding that her pure mezzo-soprano voice was well suited to folk ballads. Baez moved with her family from California to the Boston area in 1958 just as the folk music scene around Harvard University was burgeoning, with coffee houses—many of which had previously been jazz clubs—popping up everywhere. Baez performed at Club 47, the best-known of these venues, then gained the attention of a

national audience at the first Newport Folk Festival in 1959.

Following her success at Newport, Baez immediately became a mainstay on the Greenwich Village folk scene in New York City. The combination of her striking appearance and unique voice, which Bob Dylan described as "like that of a siren from off some Greek island," ignited a bidding war between record companies. Ultimately, Baez signed with Vanguard, a small independent label, to retain the artistic control she felt she might lose with a more commercial label. Eleven of the thirteen songs on her first album, *Joan Baez*, in 1960,

18 Joan Baez with Bob Dylan in London during his 1965 tour of England, captured in the film *Don't Look Back*.

19 Joan Baez is arrested in 1967 while protesting the military draft at an induction center in Oakland, California.

recorded when she was nineteen, are traditional ballads. Baez performed them emotively, accompanied only by acoustic guitar, a direct reflection of her live performances. In her concerts, Baez seemed introspective, yet also directly engaged with her audiences; she is often described as a "mesmerizing" performer. Following Seeger's practice, she would regularly engage the audience in communal singing, teaching unfamiliar lyrics and encouraging the reluctant to join in.

Although Baez was committed to pursuing both folk music and political activism early on, the traditional ballads she favored did not speak to current realities. She found the solution to this problem in the songs of such Greenwich Village colleagues as Bob Dylan and Phil Ochs, both of whom were writing topical songs in the early 1960s. Introduced to the audience of the 1959 Newport Folk Festival by the singer Bob Gibson, Baez continued this tradition by introducing Dylan at the 1963 festival and inviting him to perform at her concerts.

Inspired by Seeger and folk singer Harry Belafonte—as well as her own Quaker family—Baez committed herself to social justice and pacifism. Like many others on the Greenwich Village scene, she was active in the civil rights movement, performing "We Shall Overcome" during the March on Washington in 1963 at which Reverend Martin Luther King Jr. gave his historic "I Have a Dream" speech. Two years later, Baez returned to Washington, DC, to partake in a protest against the Vietnam War and the military draft.

20 Joan Baez performs at The War Is Over! concert and peace rally quickly organized in the summer of 1975 to celebrate the end of the war in Vietnam and draw attention to the humanitarian and social issues left unresolved in its wake.

20–21 Joan Baez at The War Is Over! in New York City's Central Park, 1975.

At the invitation of the North Vietnamese, she visited Hanoi in 1972 and experienced American military action there firsthand. Over the years, she has worked for peace in war-torn countries throughout the world. Partly of Mexican heritage herself, she supported the United Farm Workers in California. On her 1974 album, *Gracias a la Vida (Here's to Life)*, Baez sang only in Spanish and stated that the recording was meant as a "message of hope" to the people of Chile.

While considered to be "folk royalty," Baez has intersected with many different audiences and genres of music over a long career. She was the last performer on the first day of the Woodstock Festival in 1969, where she performed a mix of traditional ballads, gospel songs and spirituals, civil rights anthems, and songs written by her contemporaries. In the early 1980s, she performed with the Grateful Dead. Although Baez retired from giving concerts in 2019, partly out of concern that her voice was no longer able to sustain the rigors of continual performance, she still sings at events organized to address social injustices.

FROM OPERA TO ROCK

PAT BENATAR

< Pat Benatar, whose stage outfits started a fashion trend, performs in 1980.

At the dawn of the music video era, Pat Benatar was a force to be reckoned with. She was the first female artist to be seen on MTV—her video for "You Better Run" was the second clip ever to be shown on the channel when it debuted in 1981. She won the Grammy for Best Female Rock Vocal Performance every year from 1981 through 1983, placed seventeen songs on the charts—beginning with the striking "Heartbreaker" in 1979—and sold millions of albums worldwide. Inspired to sing professionally after seeing Liza Minnelli, Benatar developed a following—and caught the attention of the music industry—

while performing regularly at a well-known comedy club in New York City.

Benatar had trained as an opera singer, and her voice was well suited to the standards she performed in night clubs. Although Benatar's management pressured her to perform ballads, she aspired to be a rock singer and worked to make her voice rougher and grittier. Benatar is acclaimed for her vocal technique—the control, precision, and expressivity she brings to rock singing, and her ability to move seamlessly across her five-octave range. Her powerful singing made her a quintessential

arena rock performer. She is considered one of the best female rock singers of all time. She is a forceful performer who assumes complete command of the stage. Benatar aligns herself with feminism, and many of her songs reflect an assertive attitude toward relationships. As she has said, "Most chick singers say, 'If you hurt me, I'll die'...I say, 'If you hurt me, I'll kick your ass.'" She takes on the difficult subject of child abuse in "Hell Is for Children" and celebrates the power and resilience of women with "Shine." Benatar was inducted into the Rock and Roll Hall of Fame in 2022.

QUEEN BEY

< Beyoncé performs in Frankfurt, Germany, during her 2007 Beyoncé Experience tour.

In 2008, Beyoncé released her third studio album, *I Am... Sasha Fierce*. The title refers to the two sides of Beyoncé's persona as a musician. "I Am" represented a quieter, more introspective side, while Sasha Fierce was an alter ego Beyoncé described as the more assertive identity she assumed when performing, the entity she became when preparing to go onstage. The two singles released from the album, "If I Were a Boy" and "Single Ladies (Put a Ring on It)," reflect the dichotomous identity around which the album was designed. Thematically, both songs are about the aftermath of a failed relationship, but

whereas the former is a wistful ballad in a pop-rock style that expresses sadness at having been mistreated, the latter is an up-tempo, electropop dance number that celebrates the woman's newfound freedom. This dual perspective had also informed the music of Destiny's Child, the R&B girl group, initially called Girl's Tyme, that Beyoncé Giselle Knowles joined in her native Houston in 1990, and with whom she performed through 2006 (although she launched her career as a solo artist in 2003 with the album *Dangerously in Love*). On the one hand, the group's song "Cater 2 U" (2004) is an expression of a

woman's loyalty to a man and her desire to give him pleasure. On the other hand, "Independent Women Part I" (2000), a #1 hit on the Billboard Hot 100, is a portrait of a woman in complete control of all aspects of her life, with particular emphasis on the fact that she maintains her independence by earning her own money. Although Beyoncé subsequently abandoned the Sasha Fierce identity saying she no longer needed it, that album and the ideas behind it speak to important aspects of her work— including her self-awareness as a performer—especially her desire to foreground female subjectivity and to portray women's social

26 Destiny's Child, the R&B girl group with which Beyoncé first achieved success, performs in Las Vegas in 2000. From left to right: Farrah Franklin, Kelly Rowland, Beyoncé Knowles, and Michelle Williams.

27 Beyoncé performs at the Made in America Festival in Philadelphia in 2015.

and emotional lives in all their complexity. In her music, Beyoncé simultaneously celebrates domesticity—the happiness she has found in her marriage to hip-hop artist and entrepreneur Jay-Z and their children—and forcefully asserts women's independence, sexuality, creativity, and self-determination. Although the tensions between the different perspectives Beyoncé presents have led some to question her commitment to feminism, others suggest that the way her songs address everyday realities enables her feminist message to reach young women, especially young Black women. She is surrounded by a coterie of deeply dedicated and active fans, most of whom are female, that she has labeled the "BeyHive." Beyoncé herself has made her stance very clear. At the 2014 MTV Music Awards, she appeared in front of a backdrop with the word FEMINIST at monumental scale behind her. Her 2013 hit single "Flawless" contains a lengthy sample from a talk by Nigerian author Chimamanda Ngozi Adichie addressing the ways girls are acculturated to be dependent on men. Beyoncé enacts her commitment to feminism through her support of female musicians. Since 2006, she has been accompanied by a ten-piece all-woman band she assembled, called the Suga Mamas. She explained her decision to showcase female musicians by saying, "I had an idea to have a lot of women on stage playing instruments, so hopefully young girls can see that, and it inspires them to play instruments." The band is not just Beyoncé's backup—members of the group are prominent on stage beside her and perform solos that place them in the spotlight. Beyoncé celebrates her musical heritage in the Queens Remix of the song "Break My Soul" from her 2022 album *Renaissance*. The track is a collaboration with Madonna; on the bridge, Beyoncé raps the names of twenty-nine Black female musicians. She has personal connections to some, such as her former collaborators in Destiny's Child and her sister Solange Knowles, while others ranging from Sister Rosetta Tharpe to Aretha Franklin to Grace Jones are inspirational figures to whom she pays tribute.

POST-HUMAN POP

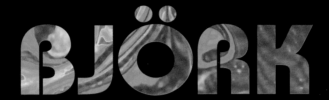

BJÖRK

< Björk in 1993, the year of her first album, *Debut*. The tattoo on her arm is the Icelandic Vegvísir, a magic symbol intended to protect travelers.

In 2011, Björk released *Biophilia*, an album addressing the idea that human beings seek connection with nature. This connection is closely related to Björk's sense of national identity; she considers nature and Iceland to be "synonymous." At the same time, she argues that because of the country's geographic isolation, contemporary Icelandic culture is shaped simultaneously by nature and technology: "We could enjoy a still almost untouched natural landscape and draw upon it as we headbutted our way into a green, techno, internet age." The importance of Icelandic

identity to Björk is illustrated by the tattoo on her left arm. This circular image, called the Vegvísir, is an Icelandic magic symbol intended to keep travelers from losing their way. It seems to guide Björk effectively as she eagerly explores an endless sonic landscape, invoking nature, magic, and technology in a spirit of restless musical innovation. Each of her albums is a different project involving distinctive instrumentation, voices, musical styles, and artistic collaborators.

Björk Guðmundsdóttir's musical talent was recognized at an early age. She studied both classical and avant-garde music

and released her first album at the age of eleven. She first gained international recognition as a member of the Icelandic alternative rock group the Sugarcubes from 1986 through 1992. This group provided the initial context for the vocal experimentation that has been at the center of Björk's work since then. In addition to singing conventionally, she engaged in wordless vocalizations and employed various vocal sound effects, including clicks, growls, and roars. Launching her solo career in 1993, Björk moved to London and immersed herself in the club scene there. The music on her first album, *Debut*,

34 Björk in London, where she launched her solo career after the Sugarcubes, 1993.

35 Björk with the Sugarcubes, the first internationally successful Icelandic rock band, Paris, 1991.

is based on the rhythms of house music but anticipates her future work by placing her voice in a wide variety of settings that often include a bed of percussion, both physical and electronic, alongside wind instruments and strings. She frequently employs unexpected juxtapositions, such as the sparse arrangement on "Like Someone in Love," in which her soaring ballad singing is accompanied only by a harp and pervasive white noise that could be an ocean. Björk once described the Sugarcubes as a "party band," and this spirit of celebration inheres in much of the danceable music she has made since, alongside other work that is more contemplative and intimate, akin to chamber music. This music showcases Björk's orchestral and choral arrangements; she has performed regularly with string ensembles ranging from quartets to symphony orchestras, culminating in the Björk Orkestral tour of 2021–2023. The sense of intimacy in this music and her performances arises not just from the centrality of Björk's voice and sometimes highly personal lyrics, but also from the way she unifies her voice with those of other singers or instrumentalists. Her Volta Tour of 2007–2008 included a ten-piece brass section made up of Icelandic women, alongside electronic instrumentation. At times, her voice assumed the timbre of a brass instrument and melded into the texture of the horns. When she employs choral groups in her performances, she stands out from the singers visually but joins her voice with theirs, sometimes mingling with them and disappearing into the group.

Björk's desire to bring together nature, technology, and magic is reflected in her ever-changing appearance, which transforms along with her exploration of fresh sonic landscapes. She sometimes appears as a hybrid creature combining human features with those of animals or insects. In 2001, she famously wore a dress to the 73rd Academy Awards that resembled a white swan wrapped around her and pretended to lay an egg in a gesture meant to refer to fertility and maternity. She has also appeared in face masks that resemble aliens or mythic symbols and is sometimes so encased by her costumes as to be visually unrecognizable, though the voice is always unmistakably hers.

36 Björk's ever-changing onstage appearance combines features of plants, animals, and the cosmos with human form. Top row: Björk performs at the Royal Albert Hall, London, in 2016 in conjunction with the exhibition of video and digital works Björk Digital. Bottom row: Björk performs at the Spandau Citadel, Germany, in 2015 during her Vulnicura tour.

37 Björk disappears into a floral costume during Cornucopia at the Shed, New York City, 2019.

ART POP

KATE BUSH

The year 2022 was declared to be the start of a Kate Bush renaissance resulting from the popularity of her 1985 song "Running Up That Hill" following its use in the US television program *Stranger Things*. This brought fresh attention to an artist whose most recent album of new material had appeared in 2011 and who had produced only seven albums since 1982, with gaps between them as long as twelve years. At the very start of her career, in the late 1970s, Bush had waited several years to release her first album while she studied dance and mime and honed her musical skills.

Thereafter, her career trajectory seemed entirely conventional for a pop musician, with new albums coming every two years or so. Bush had been a prolific songwriter since she was a teenager, and during this period, she assumed greater control over the production of her music as well as its composition, leading up to her first entirely self-produced album *The Dreaming* (1982). Since then, she has taken a very deliberate approach to her career, releasing new music only when she feels it's ready. She also maintains a low public profile, saying at one point that she would rather devote herself to making music than to promoting it.

Bush was a distinctive and provocative performer from the start. Although it is tempting to describe her as a singer-songwriter and much of her music partakes of the intimate affect associated with the genre, her music only rarely seems to be a direct expression of her experience or feelings. Whatever Bush has to say, she says it by creating clearly fictional characters through whom to speak, characters who populate strange, often disturbing narratives with elements of myth, science fiction, romanticism, and gothic horror juxtaposed with elements of the everyday. These narratives are sometimes

40 Kate Bush performs in Amsterdam on the Tour of Life in 1979, using the headset microphone created for her by her sound engineer.

41 Kate Bush performs the song "Kite" on the Tour of Life in 1979.

inspired by literary or cinematic sources. "The Sensual World" (1989) brings James Joyce's Molly Bloom to life, while "Hammer Horror" (1978) is a tribute to the famous British film studio. The British singer Rae Morris has said of Bush, "Her music is all about combining small details with spiritual, otherworldly, wider cinemascope stuff: a really grand, imaginative to-the-moon-and-back scale, but also the sound of the blood running through your veins." As a singer, Bush is able to move very rapidly up and down her voice's registers. Over time, she has incorporated rougher vocal timbres, including screaming, into her work. As a composer and performer, she has ranged over a vast stylistic territory that includes the dense, percussive, texturally complex *The Dreaming*, achieved using the Fairlight synthesizer, and the much more open, jazz piano trio texture of *50 Words for Snow* (2011). On her debut single, "Wuthering Heights" (1978), initially inspired by a film version of the novel, Bush sings in the upper register of her pure soprano voice. Like many of Bush's songs, "Wuthering Heights" contains repeated motifs that never quite fall into a verse-chorus pattern but unfold over a constant instrumental bed of piano and strings. In the video, Bush moves in a distinctive, highly stylized fashion that incorporates elements of dance and mime and expresses the emotions of the song through wide-eyed, exaggerated facial expressions. Bush has suggested that her vocal technique evolved in tandem with her explorations of dance and movement. She elaborated this highly theatrical performance style in the Tour of Life (1979), which involved numerous costume changes, poetry, and stage magic. Bush is credited with being the first performer to use a homemade headset microphone to enable her to dance freely. The tour was successful but left Bush exhausted. Although she performed occasionally at benefit concerts and continued to make videos to accompany her music, she did not engage in extensive live performance until 2014, when she made an unexpected return to the stage for a series of concerts she titled Before the Dawn, which deployed songs from her entire career over a three-act dramatic structure. Bush enjoys a devoted international fan base that celebrates the Most Wuthering Heights Day Ever in her honor annually and the admiration of fellow musicians ranging from Björk to hip-hop artist Big Boi of Outkast.

TALKIN' BOUT A REVOLUTION
TRACY CHAPMAN

< Tracy Chapman performing in Paris in 1998, with her acoustic guitar as her only accompaniment.

When Tracy Chapman's "Fast Car" burst onto the radio in 1988, it sounded like nothing else at the time. Through the song's direct, first-person narrative of a working-class woman in a dead-end job seeking escape to a better life and the unadorned style of the music, Chapman brought new life to the singer-songwriter genre. She also brought the perspective of an African American woman, a voice heard all too infrequently in this context. Chapman experienced poverty and racism firsthand as a child in Cleveland, Ohio. "It was a difficult place, for me, to grow up," she has said. "It was a very racially divided city, and in most places public schools were forced to desegregate, and white people

protested and tried to stop buses. That was a controversial time. We always had trouble." She was aware of being poor and disenfranchised, but also of the social and political reasons for her situation. Chapman came up through the folk music scene in Cambridge, Massachusetts, which had also nurtured Joan Baez a generation earlier, where she performed in clubs and as a busker. Possessed of a rich contralto voice, her emotional palette is broad. Although the marginalized characters in Chapman's songs reflect her own experience, they are fictional creations. She explains, "In songs, you take on different personas and different characters, and try and put yourself in their place." The social engagement

Chapman expresses in her music led immediately to her being invited to appear at high-profile social justice–related gigs, such as Nelson Mandela's 70th birthday concert at Wembley Stadium and 1989's Amnesty International tour. Chapman does not aspire to be a public figure, however. From 1988 through 2009, she recorded eight albums and toured extensively, but she has maintained a low profile since. Chapman broke her silence in 2020, on the eve of the American presidential election. She performed her song "Talkin' Bout a Revolution" on television with the ending altered to encourage people to vote, saying, "It is imperative that everyone vote to restore our democracy."

POP DIVA

< Cher in 1979.

When told by her mother that she should marry a rich man to have the means to pursue her goals, Cher blurted out, "Mom, I am a rich man!" For Cher, this statement is a declaration of female autonomy, an autonomy she admits is hard-won. Born Cherilyn Sarkisian, she moved on her own to Los Angeles in 1962 at age sixteen with a desire for fame and no clear idea of how to achieve it. She took acting classes, performed in clubs, did some work as a backup singer, and networked relentlessly. She met Salvatore "Sonny" Bono, then working for record producer Phil Spector, at the end of that year. Bono saw

Cher as a solo artist; suffering from stage fright, she asked him to sing with her. The result was a dual career for Cher as part of the duo Sonny and Cher and as an artist in her own right. In August 1965, she was both at #1 on the Billboard Hot 100 with Sonny and Cher's breakthrough hit "I Got You Babe" and at #18 with her version of Bob Dylan's "All I Really Wanna Do."

This early phase of Cher's career already demonstrated her considerable versatility. Whereas "All I Really Wanna Do" and her first albums were in a style related to the folk-rock rapidly developing in Los Angeles, her 1966 single "Bang Bang (My

Baby Shot Me Down)" showed her skill at pop melodrama. For "You Better Sit Down Kids" (1967), Cher sang from the perspective of a man trying to explain his impending divorce to his children. Cher's low contralto voice, unusual in the context of popular music, was sometimes perceived as male. This musical androgyny was reflected in the unisex clothing Sonny and Cher wore, some of which Cher made herself, which proved influential on youth fashion. Arguably, Cher helped make ambiguous gender identity more visible and palatable to a mainstream audience.

Television was one of the media through which

46 Cher in a mini-dress for a television guest appearance in 1967.

47 Sonny and Cher on the set of *The Sonny and Cher Comedy Hour* in the early 1970s.

48-49 Cher and her digital duplicate, the visual parallel to her use of Auto-Tune, on stage in Germany in 1999.

49 Cher in the costume she wore in the music video for "If I Could Turn Back Time," 1989.

Cher reached this audience in the 1970s, with *The Sonny and Cher Comedy Hour* and her own variety show, *Cher*. In both, she was showcased in fashions that turned her into a symbol of glamour.

Despite her success in pop music, Cher aspired to be a rock singer, an ambition to which she has returned periodically. In 1969, as the kind of pop music with which she was associated became unfashionable, Cher released the rock album *3614 Jackson Highway*. Although critically acclaimed, it was not commercially successful. With Gregg Allman, Cher recorded the soulful album *Two the Hard Way* in 1977. She made another foray into rock as the singer for the band Black Rose in 1980. At the same time, she ventured into disco, reluctantly at first, and found a home in dance music. In the 1980s, Cher focused largely on film acting, culminating in a Best Actress Oscar for *Moonstruck* (1987).

Cher has said that she experiments with musical styles to "remain relevant and do work that strikes a chord." In 1998, she achieved surprising new relevance through technological innovation. Her #1 song "Believe" is the first recording to make use of Auto-Tune, a pitch-correction software program, not to cover up mistakes but as a deliberate artistic device, paving the way for the overt use of Auto-Tune by other artists, particularly in hip-hop.

Cher observes that whereas she had to make compromises early on, her remarkable professional longevity has given her the power to determine her own course: "I tailored myself and I adjusted myself and then I got tired of adjusting myself. But I realized that when you have no power, it's difficult to stand your ground and after you've been in a job for 60 years, or however long I've been doing this, then you can just tell everybody that you're going to do what you want to do."

HEAVY METAL QUEEN

There is currently ample evidence that female musicians participate in the genre of heavy metal, including online lists of the 100 Greatest Female Singers in Heavy Metal. Young women in the genre now have a history of progenitors and role models on which to draw. It was not always this way. Though there were important female heavy rock pioneers in the late 1960s and early 1970s, including Janis Joplin, the Runaways (from which emerged Joan Jett and guitarist Lita Ford), Pat Benatar, and Suzi Quatro, heavy metal evolved during the same period as an entirely male-dominated genre.

Two developments changed this picture. The first was the appearance of glam metal in the early 1980s, largely in Los Angeles. Performers in this subgenre adopted androgynous looks that challenged the machismo of heavy metal and provided a point of entry for female musicians and bands. The second is the second wave of British heavy metal, which also became visible in the early 1980s. Although the gender politics of this scene were still male dominated, it was inclusive enough to inspire huge numbers of young musicians to form bands, some of which had prominent female members.

This was the situation into which Doro (Dorothee Pesch), who always appears at the top of lists of important women in heavy metal, entered in 1983 when she became the lead singer and frontwoman for the German metal band Warlock, based in her hometown of Düsseldorf. The group issued its first album, *Burning the Witches*, the next year and started relentlessly touring Europe and the UK. A 1986 appearance at the annual Monsters of Rock heavy metal festival at Castle Donington in the UK alongside such established acts as Def Leppard and Motörhead cemented the group's status within the heavy

> Doro onstage at Halle 101, Speyer, Germany, in 2014.

metal community. Doro has said that this event was the first time she became aware of being the only woman onstage. She was, in fact, the first woman to perform at this festival. Nevertheless, she insists that she never felt excluded from the heavy metal fraternity. "I always felt really accepted…[the male musicians] were all very supportive…It didn't really matter that I was a woman or where I was from." In 1988, Warlock embarked on the group's only tour of the US, opening for Megadeath. During this tour, the band's personnel changed entirely, leaving Doro as the only German member. Doro and the new group entered the recording studio to produce the next Warlock album but left instead with Doro's

52 Doro performing in the UK in 2009 with bassist Nick Douglas and guitarist Joe Taylor, both members of her band at the time.

53 Doro performing in Germany in 2014.

first record as a solo artist, *Force Majeure*, released in 1989. She continues to record and perform regularly, both under her own name and as Warlock. She was the first heavy metal artist to perform a drive-in concert in 2020 during the COVID-19 pandemic. Doro's powerful, coarse-grained voice lends itself equally well to the declamatory style of heavy metal singing appropriate to such up-tempo yet ominous songs as "I Rule the Ruins" and "Burning the Witches," which evokes ritual violence, and to more melodic power ballads like the inspirational pledge of loyalty "Für Immer" ("Forever"), the only song Warlock recorded in German. Doro is a tireless advocate for her genre and the community surrounding it, as reflected in songs such as "We Are the Metalheads." In performance, she plays the role of heavy metal frontperson to the hilt. Dressed in black leather (no longer real, as she has become an animal activist), she stalks the stage, headbangs, pumps her fists, throws up the "devil horns" hand sign, and works the audience, encouraging them to sing along. She is aggressive, but not threatening, and always joyful. In Doro's hands, heavy metal music is not dark, no matter how portentous the lyrics may be, but festive and triumphant.

BILLIE EILISH

< Billie Eilish arrives at the 2021 MTV Video Music Awards in New York City.

In Billie Eilish's music videos, she appears as an isolated and often beleaguered figure, whether it's the restless soul looking for something to do at home in "Male Fantasy," the woman subjected to what seems to be medical experimentation in "Bury a Friend," or the oil-covered, bat-winged angel of "All Good Girls Go to Hell." The exclusive focus on these solitary, troubled characters in the videos constitutes a kind of intimacy, though it is not necessarily an intimacy the characters seem to welcome. Consequently, it often feels like we are intruding.

Eilish's lyrics provide entry into a hermetic world of characters who feel abandoned and resentful or celebrate their own destructive and antisocial behaviors and their desire for power over others. The musical arrangements and production of her recordings place her voice squarely in the foreground. Eilish's voice is breathy, yet strong and can sound alternately wistful, dreamy, longing, or angry. On her recordings and in live performance, her voice is sometimes distorted to sound otherworldly or multitracked to amplify the characters' disturbing thoughts.

Instrumentation is spare and ranges from thumping dance beats to folkish acoustic guitar. It serves primarily to provide atmospheric settings for the characters' ruminations. Although Eilish achieves an effect of intimacy through her songs' confessional narratives and the closeness of her voice, her characters' thoughts should not be confused with her own. "It's really fun to put yourself into a character—into shoes you wouldn't normally be in," she has said. "You don't have to be in love with someone to write a song about being in love with someone. You don't have to hate somebody to write

56 Billie Eilish performs at the 2019 Summerfest Music Festival in Milwaukee.

57 Billie Eilish performs at the 2021 iHeart Music Festival in Las Vegas.

a song about hating somebody. You don't have to kill people to write a song about killing people. I'm not going to kill people, so I'm just going to become another character."

As in her videos, Eilish often appears alone in her live performances, a single figure on a large stage. She frequently seems introspective, absorbed in her own world and feelings. Eilish lies down on the stage, sits, lowers her head, and crouches. At these moments, she casts her audience in the role of voyeur; it is as if we are looking in on her at very private moments. At other points, she is buoyant, dashing athletically around the stage, leaping up and down, and engaging her audience in singalongs. At all times, she is clearly very conscious of her fans and of her power to construct her relationship with them.

In a short film titled "Not My Responsibility," which Eilish sometimes shows as an interval during her concerts, she seems to disrobe while directly expressing her hyper-awareness of being watched in voice-over. She simultaneously takes off her clothes and critiques her audience's desire to see her body. As a very young performer seeking to define herself, Eilish uses clothing strategically to retain a modicum of privacy in the face of the invasive public scrutiny that has only intensified in the age of social media.

58–59 Billie Eilish leaps in the air while performing at Madison Square Garden in New York City on her Happier Than Ever tour, 2022.

59 Billie Eilish and her brother and musical collaborator, Finneas, perform at Coachella, 2022.

Eilish's fashion choices are distinctive and influential. She has a penchant for unrevealing baggy clothes, such as T-shirts and skater pants drawn from the Southern Californian environment in which she grew up. This aesthetic has been interpreted positively as her resisting the ways the entertainment industry objectifies women and subjects them to normative gender definitions. At the same time, her influence as a rising star has induced designers to produce clothing that echoes Eilish's looks, turning them into a fashion trend. Ultimately, Eilish equates control over her appearance with autonomy in defining her gender identity, stating, "I feel like I'm capable of being as feminine as I want to be and as masculine as I want."

ROOTS ROCKER

MELISSA ETHERIDGE

< Melissa Etheridge performs on the twelve-string guitar at the Tempodrom, Berlin, during her Live and Alone tour of 2002.

Growing up in Kansas, Melissa Etheridge was a serious student of the guitar whose teacher and parents encouraged her to pursue her interest. She matriculated at the Berklee College of Music in Boston but could not find her place there. "I was one of two female guitar players there," she has said. "The classroom had 60 guitar players, and I kind of felt lost." Etheridge moved to Los Angeles to build a career as a singer-songwriter and found her audience in lesbian bars. Word got out, she attracted the attention of the music industry, and she released her well-received debut album in 1988.

Etheridge is often compared with Bruce Springsteen as an artist who represents the emotional honesty, direct address, and unadorned style prized in classic rock. Feeling that the truthfulness she sought in her songwriting was not matched by her public persona, she came out as a lesbian in 1993 and became a vocal supporter of the LGBTQ+ community. Etheridge's song "Come to My Window" has become an LGBTQ+ anthem. In another example of her openness with her audience, she performed at the 2005 Grammy Awards with her head bald from the treatments she was undergoing for breast cancer.

Etheridge's songs frequently convey the complexity of romantic relationships. Her voice is husky and deep; she sings with the energy and passion of a soul singer. On songs such as "The Only One" and "Come to My Window," her performances build in burning intensity up to choruses where she unleashes the full power of her voice. Etheridge has never lost her devotion to the guitar, an instrument she clearly loves. Although she initially did not play solos on her recordings, she has become an accomplished rock and blues guitarist. In 2016, she embarked on her This Is M.E. solo tour, which showcased her instrumental skills. Surrounded onstage by guitars, she used a looping device to multitrack her instruments and voice in real time, selecting exactly the right guitar for each song and playing beautiful solos with concentration and depth.

ARETHA FRANKLIN

< Aretha Franklin
in 1967, the year of
"Respect" and the
beginning of her reign
as the Queen of Soul.

In the late 1960s, Aretha Franklin was crowned the Queen of Soul by Chicago radio personality Pervis Spann on the stage of the Regal Theater. Always a commanding performer, she reigned as undisputed soul royalty for the next half-century.

Franklin grew up in a household whose atmosphere was suffused with music and social activism. Her father, the Reverend C. L. Franklin, a prominent Detroit pastor and civil rights activist, himself a singer, took her with him on his tours around the United States. Her first recordings as a fourteen-year-old prodigy, made in 1956, were of gospel music. Although Franklin switched from sacred to secular music at the age of eighteen, moving to New York City to record for Columbia Records, her most successful music retained the depth and fervor of gospel. Her celebrated 1972 album *Amazing Grace*, recorded with a choir, marked a return to performing sacred music, but her earlier hits, beginning with "I Never Loved a Man (The Way I Love You)" in 1967, had fused gospel with rhythm and blues. She built secular songs on a gospel foundation and revealed the sanctified in other artists' music. Her 1972 version of the Beatles' "The Long and Winding Road," recorded with the classic gospel instrumentation of organ and piano against swelling choral vocals, turns the homecoming narrative into a quest for grace.

Columbia proved unable to find the right musical context for Franklin, despite releasing nine albums with her. In 1967, when her contract with Columbia ran out, she moved to Atlantic Records. Whereas Columbia had sought to mold Franklin to fit into existing marketable genres as a jazz and blues singer, Jerry Wexler, her producer at Atlantic, encouraged her to create her own style with her singing and piano playing at its center. Franklin took control in the studio, making clear to the male session musicians that

64 Aretha Franklin in 1964, already an accomplished jazz, blues, and gospel singer at age twenty-two.

65 Aretha Franklin in 1978, at the time of the recording sessions for her album *Almighty Fire.*

66–67 Aretha Franklin onstage at the New Victoria Theatre, London, in 1980.

she was there to play. Sitting at the piano, she and her sisters, Erma and Carolyn, her musical collaborators and backup singers, worked out the feeling of a song and created vocal arrangements. Franklin embarked on a series of legendary recordings that would come to define a kind of soul music different from what was coming off the Motown production line in her native Detroit and closer in spirit to the grittier soul music coming out of Memphis. Between 1967 and 1973, fourteen of Franklin's singles went Top 10 on both the Pop and Rhythm and Blues charts in the United States. Franklin's second Atlantic single, her version of Otis Redding's "Respect," a song of which she had been a fan since it came out in 1965 and which she had started incorporating into her club performances when she was still with Columbia, went to #1 and cemented her position as the Queen of Soul. In Redding's recording, the male protagonist begs a woman for respect. Franklin sings from a woman's point of view to articulate her own ultimatum, altering the lyrics strategically to make her demand for respect much more confident and assertive than Redding's. In the last quarter of the song, Franklin abandons the narrative altogether, as she and her sisters repeatedly sing and spell out R-E-S-P-E-C-T over an increasingly propulsive rhythm. In Franklin's version, the song is no longer a negotiation between a man and a woman but becomes a demand for respect that was heard as an anthem for both the women's movement and the civil rights movement. As Franklin put it, "It was the right song at the right time." Franklin followed in her father's footsteps as a supporter of the civil rights movement, both in her music and through her actions. She undertook a benefit concert tour to support Reverend Martin Luther King Jr. and sustained the movement financially behind the scenes. Although Franklin achieved greatness through recordings made beginning in the mid-1960s, she remained a vital force through the 1980s and beyond. Her 1985 album, *Who's Zoomin' Who*, for which she turned to contemporary dance music for inspiration, was hugely successful, and in 1987, she became the first woman to be inducted into the Rock and Roll Hall of Fame. Her last public performance was at a benefit for Elton John's AIDS foundation in 2017. She died the following year.

"We all require and want respect, man or woman, black or white. It's our basic human right."

—Aretha Franklin

GODMOTHER OF PUNK
NINA HAGEN

< Nina Hagen on Hollywood Boulevard, Los Angeles, in 1978.

Although Nina Hagen had a significant influence on the German punk and new wave scene in the mid-1970s, her claim to the title of Godmother of Punk derives less from her musical style than from her outlandish and aggressive stage persona. Hagen is responsible for some archetypal punk gestures, such as her desecration of the self-congratulatory pop standard "My Way," but the Nina Hagen Band, which she formed in West Berlin in 1977, was primarily a hard rock group. In 1983, she had a hit on the dance club charts with the electro-pop "New York New York" on which she rapped the lyrics in a variety of voices. Over her long career, Hagen has worked in several rock, pop, and dance styles and has also made some surprising musical detours. Her 2003 album, *Big Band Explosion*, found her singing jazz standards while fronting the Leipzig Big Band, while *Om Namah Shivay* (1999) was devoted entirely to Hindu prayers. As a teenager, Hagen studied opera while listening to Janis Joplin and Tina Turner records smuggled into East Germany and can sing classical and cabaret music as well as rock. She has performed programs of songs by Bertolt Brecht and Kurt Weill.

Hagen originally set out to be an actress, and her musical persona reflects her theatrical bent. Often described as "chameleonic," Hagen changes her appearance continually, sometimes in the middle of a concert, particularly by changing the style and color of her hair (or wig). She is well-known for her use of heavy eye makeup, which often recalls Japanese Kabuki theater. She sings in a range of voices that includes one as squeaky and rapid as if she had inhaled helium, a power ballad voice, fearsome heavy metal growls, screams, trills, and various other noises. She employs extravagant, wide-eyed

70 Nina Hagen performing at the Ritz, New York City, in 1980.

71 Nina Hagen performs at the legendary Paris nightclub Les Folies-Bergère in 1988.

facial expressions and grimaces. A 1983 review from the *New York Times* summarizes her impact: "She ranted; she yodelled; she rapped; she growled; she sighed. She moaned like a cabaret singer and cackled like a witch; she belted like a diva and scatted up high like a modern-jazz singer. She even warbled the 'Habanera' from Bizet's *Carmen* as the band played Michael Jackson's 'Beat It.' And at every mercurial phrase, she was in complete control, vocally and theatrically." Hagen's first pop hit, "Du hast den Farbfilm vergessen" ("You Forgot the Color Film") of 1974 appears to be a sullen complaint on the part of a young woman about her male companion but was widely understood to be a critique of the bleakness of life in Communist East Germany. "The song drips with irony," Hagen says. "It plays on the huge aspiration to flee the black-and-white film to a place full of color and light." Increasingly at odds with the regime, Hagen was permitted to leave East Germany in 1977. She witnessed the birth of punk rock in London, then returned to Germany, to West Berlin, where she established a reputation for wild performances that celebrated her new-found freedom from repression.

The intense stylization of Hagen's performances should not be mistaken for ironic distance. Hagen uses her platform to articulate sincerely held political and religious beliefs. She has recorded songs that address political and social issues directly, such as animal rights in "Don't Kill the Animals," a 1986 duet with Lene Lovich; racism in "Unity," her 2020 collaboration with George Clinton in support of Black Lives Matter; and international feminism in "United Women of the World" (2022). She underwent two conversion experiences, one when she saw a UFO in Malibu and an earlier encounter with Jesus while on LSD, both of which inform her unconventional brand of Christianity. She was baptized in 2009 and regularly performs religiously themed music in her over-the-top style.

72–73 Nina Hagen performs during the 2010 Veranos de la
Villa music festival in Madrid, Spain.

KATHLEEN HANNA

The riot grrrl movement, which originated in Olympia, Washington, was a direct response to the development of grunge in neighboring Seattle. In the early 1990s, grunge drew on the energy and anarchy of 1970s punk rock. It was a heavily male dominated scene, in which female fans felt themselves to be in physical danger because of the belligerent behavior of male concert crowds. In 1991, university student Kathleen Hanna designed and self-published the second issue of her zine, *Bikini Kill.* In her "Riot Grrrl Manifesto," Hanna declared the need for a cultural space belonging to women and railed not only against the exclusionary punk scene but also against "a society

that tells us Girl = Dumb, Girl = Bad, Girl = Weak." Acting on the belief that music is a better means of reaching an audience than the written word, Hanna founded Bikini Kill in 1990. Bikini Kill's music is loud, aggressive, fast-paced punk rock that articulates feminist themes. "Double Dare Ya" goads women to assert their right to self-definition, while "Daddy's Little Girl" addresses sexual assault and exploitation. "Rebel Girl," which celebrates female solidarity and friendship, became the riot grrrl anthem. As singer and frontperson, Hanna screamed, raged, and prodded her audiences to be politically active. Her rallying cry at performances, "Girls to the front!" directly

challenged men's control and was intended to create a safe space both for women and for the band members by encouraging female fans to stand directly in front of, or even on, the stage. As Hanna has observed, reaction to Bikini Kill on the part of male spectators and musicians was frequently harsh. "We experienced our whole band within a kind of washing machine of backlash and hatred. We went through the '90s feeling physically unsafe at our *own shows*." Bikini Kill disbanded in 1997 but regrouped in 2019. In between, Hanna fronted two other groups, the Julie Ruin and Le Tigre, that set feminist polemics to more accessible and highly danceable electro-punk beats.

> Bikini Kill vocalist Kathleen Hanna (*front*) and drummer Tobi Vail (*rear*) perform with Joan Jett (*left*) at Irving Plaza, New York City, in 1994.

ATOMIC BLONDE

DEBBIE HARRY

After Debbie Harry bleached her hair, men on the streets of New York City started calling out "Hey, Blondie!" to her. Harry played into this stereotype, constructing her onstage persona as a parody of conventional femininity partly inspired by Marilyn Monroe. This idea of gender identity as a performance constructed from popular media images of women was evident in the way Harry's band, also called Blondie, drew on, but twisted, the girl group sound of the early 1960s. Their first single, "X-Offender" (1976), featured the spoken introduction and the guileless attitude of girl groups like the Shangri-Las applied to the unlikely story of a prostitute who is in love with the police officer who arrested her.

Harry and the other members of Blondie were key figures on the New York club scene of the mid-1970s. At Max's Kansas City, they mingled with pop artist Andy Warhol's entourage. Harry and Warhol became friends, and he enshrined her in a famous portrait in 1980. Describing her Blondie persona as "a living cartoon character," Harry thought of her as representing a pop art version of glamour. Through the Blondie persona, Harry performed femininity simultaneously from the heterosexual perspective and that of the drag queens she encountered in the clubs, particularly the transgender actress and Warhol superstar Jackie Curtis. Harry describes her persona by saying, "Blondie, as a character, was kind of bisexual or transsexual, and would change perspectives." She adds that the character's multiple perspectives also came from her situation as a woman fronting an otherwise all-male band: "I always felt that lyrically with these songs, I was trying to represent the guys in the band as well as myself. I was trying to speak for all of us."

Harry conceived of her stage persona as a fictional character and treated the protagonists of Blondie's songs similarly. "I approached the songs from kind of an acting perspective,"

> Debbie Harry performs with Blondie at the Hammersmith Odeon, London, in 1978, the year of the group's international breakthrough album, *Parallel Lines*.

78 Publicity portrait of Blondie around 1980. Clockwise from bottom left: Clem Burke, Frank Infante, Nigel Harrison, Jimmy Destri, Chris Stein, and Debbie Harry.

79 Debbie Harry, with Blondie, in Chicago, 1979.

she has said. "With each song, I could be a new character." The frustrated lover of "Don't Leave Me Hanging on the Telephone" has a hint of a New York accent that emphasizes her aggravation. Harry endows the stalker of "One Way or Another" with swagger and a cold, threatening gaze, while the protagonist of "Pretty Baby" is alternately exultant and defeated as she ponders the image of a young movie starlet (possibly herself). In the video for "Detroit 442," Harry, in a black leather rocker outfit, portrays the working-class character's anger and frustration at being stuck in a dead-end job and life. Rather than presenting a singular identity as a singer, Harry moves from character to character, all refracted through the Blondie persona. With Blondie, Harry navigated the fragmentation of musical styles that characterized the mid-1970s and the 1980s. When the band were regulars at the New York club CBGB in the mid-1970s, their style was akin to punk in its aggression, but self-conscious in a way that placed them at the forefront of new wave. *Parallel Lines*, the breakthrough album that made them international stars in 1978 saw them embracing a more pop-rock sound while also flirting with disco on the hit "Heart of Glass" and Eurodisco on the subsequent "Call Me" of 1980. In the late 1970s, Harry immersed herself in New York hip-hop culture, and Blondie recorded the rap-infused "Rapture" in 1980, the first rap song to reach #1 on the charts. The dissolution of Blondie in 1982 gave Harry the opportunity to carve out a solo career in which she has released five albums and continues to explore dance music and genres ranging from modern rock to avant-garde jazz. In 1989, she changed her professional name to Deborah Harry to differentiate her Blondie persona from her identity as a solo artist. The group Blondie reformed in 1997 and is still a going concern, having released its most recent album in 2017.

SHAPE SHIFTER

PJ HARVEY

In 2011, the singer-songwriter Polly Jean Harvey released her eighth album, *Let England Shake*, to critical acclaim. The album won both the Mercury Prize and the Ivor Novello Award for the best album of the year. Her next album, five years later, was *The Hope Six Demolition Project*. The songs on *Let England Shake* convey the horrors of war, focusing on the First World War. Harvey did extensive research to write the album, including investigation into the involvement of members of her own family. The songs are observational. The voices of both the folkish "All and Everyone" and the ironically up-tempo rock and roller "The Words That Maketh Murder" belong to soldiers who describe what they have seen and done on the battlefield.

The Hope Six Demolition Project addresses a government scheme in the United States to refurbish public housing in poor neighborhoods. The album opens with a straightforward rocker, "The Community of Hope," in which Harvey presents her own observations, describing what she sees while touring Ward 7 in Washington, DC. Speaking of her approach to *Let England Shake*, Harvey said, "I didn't want to tell people what to think or feel. I wanted to remain a narrator." This comment applies equally well to the documentary tone of *The Hope Six Demolition Project*. Both albums represented a turn toward historical and social concerns by an artist known for the personal tone of her work and unpredictable changes of musical style. While much of her earlier music seemed confessional and emotionally raw, she has frequently ventured into hauntingly dark, Gothic narrative fictions. Regardless of whether Harvey is singing directly from her own experience or through that of an invented character, she sings in the first person and identifies with her protagonists. Even when the voices in her songs belong to fictional characters, she says, "they all come from me. It's me imagining myself in that situation, not somebody else."

> PJ Harvey performs at the Glastonbury Festival in 2016 as part of her Hope Six Demolition Project tour.

BAND LEADER

CHRISSIE HYNDE

< A photo of Chrissie Hynde, London, 1979.

Although Chrissie Hynde is the only constant presence in the history of the Pretenders, the rock band she founded in 1979 to showcase her distinctive songwriting and singing, she insists that the group is not just her backup but a band of which she is a member. In 2014, she underlined this point by releasing *Stockholm* under her own name, her only solo album to date.

Growing up in Akron, Ohio, Hynde traveled frequently to Cleveland to attend concerts by rock and soul artists. She loved music, particularly the bands, and rock guitar. She started playing guitar but did not see herself as a musician at that point. As she puts it, "I didn't think I was going

to be a rock guitar player, because I was a girl. I would've been too shy to play with guys." Rootless after dropping out of college, Hynde moved to London in 1973, then to Cleveland in 1975, on to Paris in 1976, and finally back to London the same year. She sought out other musicians in all these places with whom to start a band, but nothing worked out. Some of the people she worked with ended up in Devo, the Clash, and the Damned, but she was bereft. Remembering this time, Hynde has said, "I wanted to be in a band so bad. [. . .] All the people I knew in town, they were all in bands. And there I was, like the real loser, you know? Really the loser." She was offered an

opportunity to record as a solo artist but turned it down and persisted in trying to form a band.

In 1976, London witnessed the punk rock revolution. Hynde recalls arriving there with albums by punk godfathers Lou Reed and Iggy Pop under her arm. Although she embraced the rawness of Reed and Pop and was propelled by the energy of the London scene, Hynde could not see herself fitting into it. Whereas the DIY aesthetic of punk deemphasized musical skill, she valued traditional musicianship. As someone who grew up admiring both rock and soul artists, she felt a connection to the music's history and was not prepared to accept that all music prior to punk was worthless.

84–85 Chrissie Hynde with the Pretenders, London, 1979. From left: bassist Pete Farndon, Hynde, guitarist James Honeyman-Scott, and drummer Martin Chambers.

85 The Pretenders performing in London in 1979.

Nevertheless, she credits the punk scene for its non-discriminatory attitude and openness to the participation of women musicians. After a long period of working with various players trying to find the right combination, Hynde put together a cohesive band. The Pretenders' eponymous first album of 1980 was an immediate success and launched Hynde and the group to international recognition. While the first iteration of the Pretenders, which lasted from 1979 till 1982, partook of a punk-inflected jittery energy combined with a measure of new wave self-consciousness, Hynde subsequently recalibrated the group's sound toward more mainstream rock. In the three albums the group has produced since 2008, including *Hate for Sale* (2020), Hynde has returned to her American roots with music that evokes rock and roll, rockabilly, and country music. The songs Hynde has written for the Pretenders over the forty-three years of the group's existence range from the aggressive and acerbic "Precious" and "Tattooed Love Boys" to the polished romantic pop of "Don't Get Me Wrong" and the inspirational power ballad "I'll Stand by You." She is a quintessential rock frontwoman, dancing and snaking her way energetically around the other musicians onstage and exuding confidence and mastery at the microphone. While her singing often suggests a detached, unsentimental stance toward her own experience and her observation of the world at large, her voice can also be warm and generous, and even sweetly romantic at times.

ROCKABILLY PIONEER

WANDA JACKSON

< Wanda Jackson as a country singer, around 1970.

Wanda Jackson began performing country music as a young teenager. She was a local celebrity in Oklahoma City and had her own radio program there by the age of fourteen. At seventeen, she toured with Elvis Presley, who encouraged her to try her hand at rockabilly, an emerging genre that combined country music with rhythm and blues. Although the prospect of performing music aimed at a young audience appealed to Jackson, she was uncertain that she had the voice for rock and roll and concerned she might lose her country audience. The song "I Gotta Know," which Jackson recorded in 1956, provided a way for her to make the transition—its verses

are in a rockabilly style, while its choruses are in a traditional country music style. Jackson notes in her autobiography that the song was "a natural segue." "I had already jumped into the male-dominated world of country, so it was only natural to take the plunge into rock and roll, too." A vibrant and assertive performer, Jackson sang with a strong Southwestern accent and a strident growling timbre; she wore glamorous, homemade dresses with fringe that swayed to amplify her movements.

Her demeanor as a performer was well-suited to the burgeoning medium of television, and she appeared frequently on early country music programs.

Although Jackson is known as the Queen of Rockabilly, her recordings in that genre were too suggestive for most radio programmers. She successfully focused on country music in the 1960s and turned to gospel music in the 1970s. Jackson imported her feisty rockabilly persona into country music with songs such as "The Box It Came In" (1965) and the up-tempo "My Big Iron Skillet" (1969). In both, she threatens a cheating spouse with physical violence and even death. Before retiring in 2021, Jackson worked with younger musicians she had influenced, including Joan Jett, who produced and performed on her last album, *Encore*.

THE QUEEN OF
ROCK AND ROLL
JOAN JETT

Until around 2020, Joan Jett did not own an acoustic guitar, let alone ever play one. Because the acoustic guitar is considered an "acceptable" instrument for a girl, it represents to Jett all the times people, including her first guitar teacher, told her that girls can't play rock and roll. Her entire career has been an ongoing rebuke to such social strictures. Having established an indelible and indisputable identity as a leather-clad female rocker over four decades, Jett released new acoustic recordings of her songs on her 2022 album *Changeup*.

Joan Marie Larkin changed her last name because she felt that "Joan Jett" better encapsulated the rock musician identity to which she aspired. As a teenager growing up in Southern California in the 1970s, she hung out at Rodney's English Disco on the Sunset Strip in Los Angeles, a club devoted to British glam rock and its attendant flamboyance. Another denizen of Rodney's, the controversial songwriter and musical entrepreneur Kim Fowley, wanted to form an all-female rock band. Both Jett and teenaged drummer Sandy West separately expressed similar interests to him, and he put them in touch with each other. Together, they created

the Runaways, recruiting singer Cherie Currie, bassist Jackie Fox, and guitarist Lita Ford. The newly formed quintet debuted at the legendary Whisky A Go Go in West Hollywood during the summer of 1975, hitting the road in the fall and touring regularly. Their 1977 tour of Japan was a triumph; Jett likened the audience response to Beatlemania. By the end of 1979 the band had dissolved amidst changes of personnel and management.

The Runaways were a hard rock band and presented themselves as such on stage. For the most part unsmiling, they threw themselves into their

90 The Runaways circa 1977. From left: Cherie Currie, Joan Jett, Sandy West, Lita Ford, and Jackie Fox.

music, interacting with each other through it. Songs such as "Cherry Bomb" and "Queens of Noise" expressed female aggression and sexuality in ways not heard before in rock music. Fowley's emphasis on sexuality in his marketing of the group was highly questionable, considering that the Runaways were all only fifteen or sixteen at the start. Jett feels the recognition of young women's desire the band demanded was important, but also that the stressing of their sexuality detracted from appreciation of their musicianship. "We wanted to be sexual and that was definitely part of our identity," she has said. "But nobody paid attention to the fact that we could actually play; that was very annoying."

Although the Runaways were underappreciated by the mainstream audience and critical establishment, they were embraced by the punk underground. In New York, they played at the definitive punk club, CBGB, and shared bills with the Ramones. Jett's own style of performing in the late 1970s and 1980s was very much in the punk mode: she snarled out her lyrics and pogoed around the stage.

91 Inductees Joan Jett and the Blackhearts perform at the Rock and Roll Hall of Fame's induction ceremony in 2015.

Jett was an inspirational figure to the feminist punk riot grrrl scene of the early 1990s, collaborating with members of the groups Bikini Kill and L7, including Kathleen Hanna.

The take-no-prisoners persona Jett developed in the Runaways is at the center of her work with her band the Blackhearts. In 1981, she recruited male musicians for the group and played a career-defining performance at the Palladium in New York City with them. With the Blackhearts, Jett has achieved the widespread acclaim that eluded the Runaways. She reached #1 on the US charts with versions of "I Love Rock and Roll," still Jett's signature song, in 1981, and "Crimson and Clover" in 1982. Her visual trademarks—black shag haircut, heavy eye makeup, and leather apparel (which is no longer real leather, due to Jett's embrace of the animal rights movement)—continue to define her image. Still touring relentlessly, Jett now performs in the stolid manner of a hard rock guitarist and singer, yet retains the punk energy and intensity that have defined her as a musician all along.

KOZMIC BLUES SINGER
JANIS JOPLIN

Janis Joplin's breakthrough performance came in 1967 at the Monterey International Pop Festival with Big Brother and the Holding Company, the San Francisco–based rock band she had joined as a singer the year before. Looking at this performance in the film *Monterey Pop*, several of the reasons why Joplin became one of the defining figures of the psychedelic rock era become apparent. One is simply the expressive power of her raspy, whisky-cured voice and the visceral energy she pours into that voice and her whole body on stage. Another is the song itself, "Ball and Chain," written by the blues great Big

Mama Thornton and performed with her permission. Thornton, Bessie Smith, and other female blues artists were Joplin's chosen predecessors, whom she revered and whose influence she acknowledged frequently. In 1970, she bought a headstone for Smith's previously unmarked grave. When Joplin first left her native Texas for San Francisco in 1963, she performed at North Beach folk clubs (she originally modeled herself on Joan Baez and other female folkies), singing primarily Smith's songs. When she returned to San Francisco in 1966, it was to become a rock singer.

Although Joplin always displayed her blues influences

proudly, she and the band reworked "Ball and Chain" into something distinctly their own by slowing the tempo, switching the key from major to minor, and using it as a vehicle to display Joplin's ability to modulate her vocal dynamics from a quiet beginning that builds slowly to maximum intensity. Her approach had been strongly influenced by the soul singer Otis Redding, who also performed at Monterey. Joplin had seen him at the Fillmore in San Francisco in 1966, attending every performance and standing close to the stage to observe everything he did. She credited Redding with helping her to understand,

> Janis Joplin, a regular on the rock festival circuit, performs at the Northern California Folk-Rock Festival in 1968.

94 Janis Joplin around 1970. A hugely influential singer, Joplin was also a hippie fashion icon who appeared in the pages of *Vogue* magazine.

95 Janis Joplin poses for a publicity photo around 1970.

97 Janis Joplin onstage at the Fillmore East in New York City, 1969. The Grateful Dead was her opening act on this occasion.

in her words, how "to push a song instead of just sliding over it." Grace Slick, singer for Jefferson Airplane, describes Joplin's performance style: "She would stomp her feet, toss her hair and go from a whisper to a full-on scream in a split second…I didn't want to go on after her."

The acclaim for Big Brother and the Holding Company's performance at Monterey garnered the band a major label recording contract. However, the amount of attention Joplin received caused tension within the group, and she left at the end of 1968. With her two subsequent bands, the Kozmic Blues Band and the Full Tilt Boogie Band (which overlapped in personnel), Joplin moved away from psychedelic rock and toward a style that was infused with blues, gospel, and Memphis soul. Although she had finished recording the 1969 album *I Got Dem Ol' Kozmic Blues Again, Mama!* before her appearance at the Woodstock Music and Art Fair, it had not yet been released. As a result, she surprised her audience there by appearing with a horn section and singing in a soul music style.

Joplin is a feminist heroine to many. Even as an artsy teenager, she was a nonconformist who flouted the gender roles of her time and rose quickly to the pinnacle of the male-dominated field of rock music, opening the door for other women. That she fueled her ride with Jack Daniels and heroin has led her to be depicted as a tragic figure. She died of an overdose while making her final album, *Pearl*, released posthumously in 1970. This album is often said to be her masterpiece, the recording on which the songs and arrangements allow her voice to shine most fully. Ultimately, however, Joplin's legacy is not as a tragic figure or cautionary tale. Rather, her legacy resides in the indelible recordings she made, the performances she gave, and her inspirational impact on subsequent generations of rock singers, both female and male. Stevie Nicks, Melissa Etheridge, Florence Welch of Florence and the Machine, and Pink number among her acolytes, as do Robert Plant of Led Zeppelin and Rob Halford of Judas Priest.

"All of a sudden, someone threw me
in front of this rock and roll band.
And I decided then and there that was
it. I never wanted to do anything else."

—Janis Joplin

HIT A HIGH NOTE

ALICIA KEYS

When Alicia Keys hosted the Grammy Awards Show in 2019, she performed a segment titled "Songs I Wish I Wrote," in which she paid tribute to a host of primarily African American composers and musicians ranging from the nineteenth-century ragtime composer Scott Joplin to soul icon Roberta Flack to rapper Juice WRLD. This performance provided a catalogue of the influences and interests Keys brings together in her own music, which combines classic soul and contemporary R&B with elements of funk and hip-hop, all refracted through the sensibility of a

genre's emphasis on personal expression. The opening track of her second album, *The Diary of Alicia Keys* (2003), addresses the listener directly and promises that the songs to follow will have the intimacy of diary entries. As a performer, Keys alternates between concerts that center on her singing at the piano with more elaborately staged events that incorporate soul and hip-hop choreography and pop spectacle. One of the figures Keys mentioned at the Grammy show was Nat King Cole, the jazz balladeer and pianist. In her song "Nat King Cole

Cole to exemplify two values she stresses repeatedly and seeks to convey in her songwriting: truth to oneself and timelessness. For Keys, the jazz, soul, and hip-hop from which she takes inspiration are timeless, a quality she hopes to infuse in her own music.

Alicia Augello Cook began singing and playing the piano at an early age. "I fell in love with the piano," she has said. "I knew

> Alicia Keys performs onstage in London, 2008,

100 Alicia Keys performs the opening sequence of her Freedom tour in Detroit, 2010, during which she is released from a cage while singing "Caged Bird/Love Is Blind."

100–101 Alicia Keys performs during the 2010 BET Awards in Los Angeles.

She grew up in Hell's Kitchen, a dangerous neighborhood in New York City. She credits this environment with instilling in her the toughness and self-reliance necessary to survive in the music industry as well as an appreciation of diverse cultures and people. She celebrates New York City as a source of inspiration and opportunity, notably in "Empire State of Mind" (2009), a track by Jay-Z for which she provided the chorus; she performs her own version of the song regularly. As a young teenager attending a school for professional performers, Cook started to think about a career in music and cast around for a stage name. The name Keys, which came to her in a dream, resonated with her passion for the piano. After a false start, Keys broke through with her first album, *Songs in A Minor*, released in 2001 when she was twenty years old.

103–104 and 104 Alicia Keys performs in San Francisco during the 8th Annual Concert for UCSF Benioff Children's Hospital, 2017.

104 Alicia Keys greets her audience while performing at the 2019 iHeartRadio Music Festival in Las Vegas.

105 Alicia Keys performs a medley of songs by 2017 inductee Tupac Shakur (whose image is projected above her) at the 32nd Annual Rock and Roll Hall of Fame Induction Ceremony in New York City.

"Fallin'," a gospel flavored song about the ups and downs of a romantic relationship from this album, was the first of Keys's four #1 hits to date. Initially, Keys experimented with recording the album herself in her apartment, acquiring the nickname "Hit a high note" from her neighbors.

Keys often embeds individual experience into larger contexts in her songs. Her popular paean to female empowerment, "Girl On Fire" (2012), describes a young woman who is both anchored in the real world and positioned to transcend it through idealism and imagination. "Pawn It All" (2016) starts as a plea by a character who is willing to surrender all her worldly goods in exchange for a fresh start in life. The lyrics quickly shift from "I" to "we" as the song's frame of reference widens to include a world in crisis, also a theme of "Girl On Fire." At its mid-point, the song shifts to a refrain reminiscent of Curtis Mayfield's calls to social action, which reappears at the end of the song. In between, the lyrics shift back to the individual perspective, but the song's style, which combines the hand-clapping and piano accompaniment of gospel with the insistent rhythm and group singing of slave songs, suggests both the power of the collective voice and the individual's empowerment through community.

SINGER, SONGWRITER
CAROLE KING

< Carole King,
the epitome of the
singer-songwriter,
around 1973.

Carole King helped shape popular music at two crucial points in its history: the songwriting renaissance of the early 1960s and the rise of the singer-songwriter a decade later. A classically trained pianist with perfect pitch, teenaged King was determined to have a career in music. At college in New York City, King met aspiring writer Gerry Goffin, and the two began collaborating musically, with King as the composer and Goffin as the lyricist. The artists eventually married. Even with the support of a music publisher, many of their first songs were met with no success. Their fortunes changed

radically with "Will You Love Me Tomorrow" for the Shirelles, a local girl group, which rose to the top of the charts in 1960. A long string of subsequent hits established King as a key figure in Brill Building pop, named for a building in New York that housed many music publishers.

By 1967, as rock musicians focused more on composing their own music, this golden age of songwriting had come to an end, as had King's marriage to Goffin. Rather than writing songs for others to sing, King became a performing artist in her own right. Her universally acclaimed album *Tapestry* (1971) heralded both her arrival as a

performer and the dawning of the era of the singer-songwriter. King included two of her best-known earlier songs on this album, the Shirelles' "Will You Love Me Tomorrow" and "You Make Me Feel (Like a Natural Woman)," written for Aretha Franklin, reclaiming them by singing them in her own voice. Earthy in sound and intimate in feeling, the songs on *Tapestry* are underpinned by King's alternately reflective and propulsive piano playing. They cover a broad spectrum of emotions, ranging from joyful exuberance to the sadness at the end of a relationship, all from a woman's perspective.

LA CAMALEÓN

LADY GAGA

Lady Gaga, who has been described as "the first millennial superstar" in pop music, is a master of disguise whose musical style and physical appearance morph continually. Gaga's rise was meteoric: over the course of only a few years, she went from playing clubs in New York City to international stardom. Her 2008 album *The Fame* and its accompanying tour established her celebrity status.

Born Stefani Joanne Angelina Germanotta, Gaga began studying the piano at the age of four, becoming proficient at the instrument and at composing songs. As a student and working musician on the downtown New York scene, she became aware of performance art and developed the ambition to meld it with pop music. In 2007, Gaga collaborated with the club DJ and performance artist Lady Starlight, who encouraged her to embrace outrageousness in her style, as evidenced by her wearing the infamous "meat dress" designed by Franc Fernandez to the 2010 MTV Music Video Awards. Gaga took an unconventional approach to defining her star persona. Whereas most pop musicians seek to create a distinctive identity, Gaga's trademark was her constantly changing look, achieved

> Lady Gaga performs during her Enigma residency in Las Vegas, 2018.

110 Lady Gaga onstage in Perth, Australia, during her ArtRave: The Artpop Ball tour of 2014.

111 Lady Gaga performs at Lollapalooza during her Monster Ball tour of 2010.

partly through her commitment to extreme designer fashion that distorted her body and hid her face to the point where she was unrecognizable. The video for "Bad Romance" (2009) presents Gaga as at least thirteen different characters dressed in outfits designed by Alexander McQueen, ranging from an orange-haired naïf to an evil queen, none of whom resemble one another. Her musical style is similarly mutable, drawing extensively on the glam rock of the 1970s, contemporary electronic dance music, the dance music of the 1980s and 1990s exemplified by Madonna and Britney Spears, and power ballads. She has also ventured into rock and country music. Gaga demonstrated her versatility as a singer in an unexpected way when she toured and recorded with the legendary "saloon singer" Tony Bennett between 2014 and 2021, performing jazz standards. For these appearances, Gaga embodied archetypal show business glamour in slinky dresses and shared the spotlight with Bennett in a manner dramatically different from her usual hyperactive, domineering stage persona.

Gaga's performances are theatrical extravaganzas that include big, choreographed numbers, frequent costume changes, and elaborate sets and props. At the piano, she sometimes channels the rock and roll anarchy of Jerry Lee Lewis, while at other times she assumes the guise of a singer-songwriter offering up reflective ballads. Gaga speaks frequently of delving into the darker reaches of her psyche,

112 The finale of Lady Gaga's performance at the Jingle Bell Ball, London, 2013.

113 Lady Gaga performs in Washington, D.C., the last show of her Fame Ball tour in 2009.

and her performances often feature ominous gothic imagery and stylized violence. Late in her performance of "Paparazzi" at the 2009 MTV Video Music Awards, it appeared that blood was flowing from a wound in her chest. She was hoisted aloft by her dancers and ended the song hanging in the air limp, bloodied, and seemingly dead.

Gaga cultivates an intimate relationship with her fans, whom she calls "Little Monsters," referring to herself as the "Mother Monster." Her use of the term "monster" is meant to refer to people who feel themselves to be socially marginalized. She speaks to her concert audiences of her desire that her performances be considered safe, inclusive spaces. She champions the LGBTQ+ community in ways that include the song "Born This Way" (2011), a rousing assertion of queer identity, and featuring transsexual dancers in her troupe. She invited a gay friend to propose marriage to his boyfriend onstage during a concert in 2014. In her own performance of queer identity, Gaga has appeared as a drag king alter ego called Jo Calderone, who first surfaced as a model in the pages of *Vogue Hommes Japan* in the summer of 2010, then stood in for Gaga at the 2011 MTV Video Music Awards to accept the award in her place, claiming to be her lover. Calderone is also in the video for "Yoü and I" (2011), a country-flavored song, in which he sits atop Gaga's piano in a field while a female Gaga, who appears as a plainly dressed blonde, serenades him. Since 2015, Lady Gaga has focused increasingly on film and television acting.

SYNTH-POP SUPERSTAR
ANNIE LENNOX

< Annie Lennox in
Cologne, Germany, 1985.

Annie Lennox is best-known as the singer and dynamic center of Eurythmics, her creative partnership with guitarist Dave Stewart. In the late 19th century, Swiss comp oser Émile Jacques-Dalcroze developed eurythmics as an approach to teaching music through physical movement. Lennox had experienced eurythmics as a child; its open-ended and playful approach seemed to be a good point of reference for Lennox and Stewart's experimental ambitions. They conceived Eurythmics not so much as a group but as a project that would enable them to explore different genres and musical pathways, working with other musicians as necessary to flesh

out the concepts they developed. Beginning with synthesizer-heavy electropop, Eurythmics ventured into many different styles of music over the course of the 1980s that included elements of psychedelic rock, new wave, 60s pop, and even folk. Their breakthrough came in 1983 with their second album, *Sweet Dreams (Are Made of This)*, which they recorded in their small home studio, driven by the international success of the eponymous single.

Lennox and Stewart were highly aware of the importance of creating compelling visual images to convey their artistic vision, especially in the age of music video. Lennox assumed numerous guises both in videos and onstage,

notably through her gender-bending androgyny and her portrayals of an ever-shifting array of characters that changed along with Eurythmics' genre-shifting music. In the video for "Sweet Dreams (Are Made of This)," Lennox appears with short, vivid red hair in a male business suit, yet her face is fully made up. For the 1984 Grammy Awards, Lennox took on a drag-king image as an Elvis-like throwback to the 1950s, with black hair in a pompadour and sideburns. By contrast, she appears in the video for the joyous romantic ballad "There Must Be an Angel (Playing with My Heart)" (1985) as ethereally feminine, with long blonde hair and a simple white dress.

118 Annie Lennox performing with Eurythmics, Chicago, 1984.

119 Eurythmics performing in Chicago, 1984. From left: Dave Stewart and Annie Lennox.

Before forming Eurythmics, Lennox and Stewart had been members of the Tourists, a Scottish post-punk power-pop band that recorded three albums in 1979 and 1980. Lennox was from Scotland but living in London, studying classical flute at the Royal Academy of Music. She dropped out just prior to graduating because she wanted a career in popular music rather than as a classical musician. Lennox's distinctive style is already apparent in her work with the Tourists. As a performer, Lennox is highly theatrical, using crisp, exaggerated facial expressions and gestures to illustrate the lyrics she sings. Her movements are highly stylized, rhythmic, and precise. Lennox sings in the tenor range. Her voice is rich and powerful, sometimes reminiscent of soul and gospel vocalists. While her singing can be stentorian, it is often subtle and nuanced.

Lennox's collaboration with Stewart came to an end in 1989, though they would reunite for one album, *Peace*, and its attendant tour ten years later. In 1992, Lennox launched a solo career with the album *Diva*, a collection of reflective pop songs. Her follow-up, *Bare* (2003), is an intimate album that delves into the pain, anger, and self-questioning that comes with the dissolution of a difficult relationship as well as the experience of growing older. *Songs of Mass Destruction* (2007) expands the emotional landscape of *Bare* to include longing, desire, and a sense of incompleteness expressed more urgently than on the previous album. Since the 1990s, Lennox has become increasingly activist, particularly around AIDS awareness and women's issues. In 1985, Eurythmics wrote and recorded the feminist anthem "Sisters Are Doin' It for Themselves" with Aretha Franklin. Lennox included "Sing" on *Songs of Mass Destruction*, a powerful declaration of women's solidarity and empowerment that contrasts with the bleaker emotions of the other songs on the album, for which she enlisted an all-star group of female musicians to sing on the chorus.

120 Annie Lennox performs as a solo artist in a theatrical persona at the Freddie Mercury Tribute Concert for AIDS Awareness, Wembley Stadium, London, 1992.

121 Annie Lennox, in male drag, performs with Eurythmics, reunited to promote their *Ultimate Collection* album in 2005.

GRUNGE QUEEN
COURTNEY LOVE

In 1983, Courtney Love (born Courtney Michelle Harrison) was briefly the singer for the Los Angeles–based band Faith No More, a position she had talked her way into by the force of her personality. With this group, Love's onstage persona was introspective. Her singing was almost monotone. She stood or crouched at the mic stand, eyes closed, seemingly absorbed into the music. Performing a few years later with her own band, her voice is a full-throttle scream as she stares at the audience, throws herself around the stage, and slashes at her electric guitar. Reflecting on her time with Faith No More, she has said, "There was no place for a woman in that world. There was none. I declared that I was going to start a band. I wanted to have an all-female band that took over the entire world." By 1989, she had taken great strides toward this goal with her band, Hole, all female save for a male guitarist.

At the start of the 1980s, Love was peripatetic and in search of an identity. Having spent some time hanging out with rock musicians in London, she came home wanting to be in a band. In 1988, she taught herself to play the guitar and moved to Los Angeles, where she recruited the members of Hole by auditioning musicians who responded to advertisements she had placed. The inspiration for the group's name came from a line in Euripides's *Medea* in which the titular character refers to her inner emptiness, a theme that recurs in the lyrics to Hole's songs. The group initially played clubs around Los Angeles, venturing occasionally into the Pacific Northwest. By 1991, on the strength of their first album, they toured extensively, both nationally and internationally.

Hole's first album, the critically well-received *Pretty on the Inside* (1990) is a take-no-prisoners affair: the sound is loud and abrasive, combining punk aggression with the slower tempi and thick textures of heavy metal. The dominant emotion is rage against all the people who have

> Courtney Love rehearses with Hole for the 1995 MTV Video Music Awards show in New York City. Love dedicated the song "Violet" to her late husband, Kurt Cobain of Nirvana, and others who had died from drug overdoses.

124 Courtney Love performing with Hole at the Music Midtown Festival, Atlanta, 1999.

125 Photo of Hole, London, 1998. From left: Melissa Auf der Maur (bass), Courtney Love (guitar and vocals), and Eric Erlandson (guitar).

contributed to the emptiness and despair driving the characters in Love's seemingly autobiographical songs to the brink. The monotone voice in which Love sang with Faith No More now stands for the numbness of existential anguish. From there, Love builds up to screaming demands to be heard. Although Love's lyrics pack a powerful visceral punch, they are sufficiently abstract—and sometimes surrealist—to be open to a wide array of interpretations. The group's second album, *Live Through This* (1994), moves away from the punk impulses of the first toward a more conventional rock style that includes gentler acoustic guitar textures. Love no longer howls and snarls, but her vocal delivery and lyrics are as abrasive and pointed as ever as she presents a thoroughly unglamorous perspective on motherhood in "Plump," addresses sexual assault in "Asking for It," and excoriates the ways social pressures rob women of the ability to determine their own identities in "Doll Parts" and "Miss World."

Because Hole was based in Los Angeles, the group was not directly a part of the Seattle grunge scene or the riot grrrl scene in the Pacific Northwest, yet it has clear affinities with both, and Love is frequently nominated the Queen of Grunge. An avowed feminist, Love's mission to create a hard rock, punk-oriented band consisting of women and addressing women's experiences and anger clearly aligns Hole with riot grrrl. But Love does not affiliate herself with riot grrrl ideology. She destabilizes gender identity by averring that rock is masculine and that women can participate in its masculinity. She has said, "I like there to be some testosterone in rock and it's like, I'm the one in the dress who has to provide it!"

QUEEN OF POP

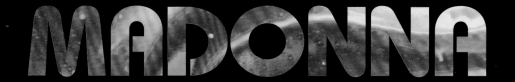

MADONNA

An ambitious musician who never shies away from experimentation or controversy, Madonna Louise Veronica Ciccone has proven herself repeatedly over her forty-year career to be a driving force in popular music. A denizen of New York City's dance clubs in the late 1970s, Madonna first made her presence known through dance music, a form in which she has worked throughout her career alongside her success on the pop charts. From 1982 through 2019, she has placed an unmatched fifty songs on the Billboard Dance Club Songs chart, a feat celebrated by the release of the anthology *Finally Enough Love* in 2022. More than once, Madonna

has brought mainstream attention to subcultural music and dance styles, beginning in the 1980s with disco, an often-dismissed genre that was nevertheless popular in the clubs. Her first dance hit, "Everybody" (1982), extolls the joys of movement with a percolating disco bass line. On her 1998 album *Ray of Light*, Madonna drew on electronica and techno, combining electronic sound with pop melodies and conventional instrumentation such as guitars and keyboards.

One of the best-known examples of Madonna's tapping into subcultural styles is "Vogue" (1990), which drew on a type of dance developed by Black

and Latin dancers in the drag queen "House Balls" of Harlem. Madonna made this community and its cultural practices more visible not only through her song but also by featuring dancers and choreographers from the community in its attendant video and on her Blond Ambition tour. Madonna's engagement with voguing proved controversial, however. While some applauded her recognition of a vital subculture that was unacknowledged because of the race and sexuality of its participants, others accused her of appropriating and gentrifying it. A later song in which Madonna borrows from another culture, "Batuka" (2019),

127

132 and 133 Madonna performs during the opening sequence of her Re-Invention tour of 2004 in Inglewood, California.

celebrates batuque, a style of drum music from Cape Verde performed by women. The song is driven by the rhythm of the Batukadeiras Orchestra, a female drum collective. In the video, Madonna joins in with them. She is dressed differently from them, not to make her the star of the video as much as to suggest that she is not making a claim on their culture.

Madonna's understanding of the power of visual imagery is clear from her frequently provocative music videos. The lyrics to her gospel-infused song "Like a Prayer" (1989) can refer equally well to religious ecstasy and sexual attraction, implying that there is an erotic dimension to religion. The video for the song includes a narrative in which a Black man is falsely accused of an assault on a white woman. Madonna witnesses the event, and her testimony secures his release. During this sequence, shots of a gospel choir are intercut with Madonna singing against a background of burning crosses, a pointed reference to the way Christian iconography has been pressed into the service of racism.

Madonna's 2019 album, *Madame X*, finds her addressing current events. The song "I Rise" is about surviving and transcending oppression. The video for it is dense with images of contemporary social flashpoints, such as school shootings, racism, homelessness, and LGBTQ+ issues, some of which are images of conciliation. The problems seem overwhelming, yet the song offers hope. By contrast, "God Control" is an explicit call for gun regulation that is much less optimistic. The video returns Madonna to where she started, a nightclub where disco music plays for the dancers. The story is told in reverse chronology. It opens with a massacre, as a gunman mows down the dancers, including a figure played by Madonna, then moves back in time to the beginnings of the evening's festivities. All the while, another woman, also played by Madonna, sits at a typewriter trying to understand the events around her but throwing out sheet after sheet of paper on which she tries to write explanations and solutions.

FORCES OF NATURE

CHRISTINE MCVIE and STEVIE NICKS

When asked how she felt about Stevie Nicks joining Fleetwood Mac in 1975, Christine McVie, who had been in the group for five years at that point, responded: "It was critical that I got on with her because I'd never played with another girl. But I liked her instantly. She was funny and nice but also there was no competition. We were completely different on the stage to each other and we wrote differently too."

Fleetwood Mac has a long and complicated history as a group, evolving from an all-male British blues band fronted by guitar legend Peter Green in the mid-1960s into one of the most successful pop-rock bands of all time in which two women, the English McVie and the American Nicks, played pivotal roles. McVie, who started her musical career on the British blues scene, and Nicks, whose early experience was in Southern Californian folk and psychedelic rock bands, represent different musical strands that, woven together, define the classic Fleetwood Mac sound first heard on two enormously successful albums, *Fleetwood Mac* (1975) and *Rumours* (1977). The latter is #7 on *Rolling Stone*'s list of the 500 Greatest Albums of All Time.

In 1968, McVie, then called Christine Perfect, brought her

"We felt like, together, we were a force of nature. And we made a pact, probably in our first rehearsal, that we would never accept being treated as second-class citizens in the music business. That when we walked into a room we would be so fantastic and so strong and so smart that none of the uber-rockstar group of men would look through us. And they never did."

—Stevie Nicks

accomplished keyboard playing and smoky alto voice to Chicken Shack, a British blues band with which she achieved some acclaim. She left the group after two years when she married John McVie, the bass player for Fleetwood Mac, which she joined in 1970. Over the next several years, McVie wrote and served as lead vocalist on many of the group's songs. She relocated from London to Los Angeles with the group in 1974. There, Lindsey Buckingham and Stevie Nicks joined Fleetwood Mac. Personal as well as musical partners at the time, they had both been in Fritz, a moderately successful psychedelic rock band, and made a more folk-rock-inflected album as a duo.

McVie and Nicks complemented one another as performers as well as songwriters. In her role as the group's keyboard player, McVie was positioned off to one side of the stage. When she took a lead vocal, she sang straightforwardly and directly, with little dramatization. By contrast, Nicks, who performed as a singer, was positioned at center stage and was much more theatrical, singing with great intensity and floating and whirling across the stage, layers of gauzy material moving with her. The differences in their styles as songwriters gave the group's material range and depth. Whereas McVie's songs are generally upbeat, based in the blues with strong pop hooks, Nicks's are more introspective and folk-oriented, with poetically evocative lyrics. As songwriters, McVie and Nicks are responsible for many of the group's most beloved tunes, including Nicks's "Rhiannon," "Landslide," and "Dreams" (the group's only #1 hit) and McVie's "Over My Head," "You Make Loving Fun," and the anthemic "Don't Stop." In addition to their work with the group, both McVie and Nicks have had substantial careers as solo artists. Nicks was the first woman to be inducted into the Rock and Roll Hall of Fame twice—once as a member of Fleetwood Mac and once on her own.

Although McVie and Nicks made their respective contributions to Fleetwood Mac as individuals, they formed an enduring friendship and an alliance to endure the rigors of touring and confront the double standards and lack of respect women face both in the male-dominated music industry and in their own band. After McVie retired from Fleetwood Mac in 1998, Nicks would dedicate songs to her when performing, referring to her as "My mentor. Big sister. Best friend." McVie returned to Fleetwood Mac in 2014. She passed away in 2022 at the age of seventy-nine.

PROTEAN GENIUS
JONI MITCHELL

> Contact sheet of portraits of the singer-songwriter Joni Mitchell, 1968.

In the summer of 2022, Joni Mitchell made a triumphant appearance at the Newport Folk Festival after not having performed in public for over two decades. She held court and sang many of her most famous songs with Brandi Carlile, who had organized the event, and a horde of other musicians paying their respects to her. Mitchell, born Roberta Joan Anderson, had become a fixture on the Canadian folk music scene by 1964. In 1967, she moved to New York City and found her footing in Greenwich Village folk clubs. She appeared initially at Newport that year, at the behest of the singer Judy Collins, who was the first to record Mitchell's "Both Sides Now" and wanted to bring attention to her as a songwriter.

As a performer, Mitchell was in many ways the quintessential folk singer, strumming an acoustic guitar and singing in a soprano that tripped lightly across registers. From the start of her career, however, she performed primarily songs she had written rather than traditional songs. Although she would maintain the stripped-down style of her folk performances, accompanying herself on an acoustic guitar, piano, or dulcimer, over her first five albums, there were also hints that her musical ambitions extended beyond the conventions of folk music, such as her use of an electric piano on "Woodstock" and of conga drums and almost doo-wop-style backing vocals on "Big Yellow Taxi." *For the Roses* (1972) is a pivotal album in which songs performed in Mitchell's folk style rub shoulders with others on which woodwinds, percussion, and syncopated rhythms reach toward folk rock and jazz. Mitchell's *Court and Spark* (1974), a California-flavored folk-rock album, initiated a period of expectation-defying musical exploration that lasted over thirty years and would see Mitchell investigate rock, jazz, and pop idioms, and instrumentation that included

140–141   Joni Mitchell at a fashion shoot for *Vogue* magazine, 1968.

strings, winds, synthesizers, and samplers. Mitchell collaborated with jazz great Charles Mingus on her contemplative 1979 album named for him. In sharp contrast, she took on the identity of a nightclub singer performing standards and some of her own songs against lush orchestral backgrounds for *Both Sides Now* (2000). She toured constantly through the year 2000; it is not surprising that her retrospective album of 2002 is titled *Travelogue*. Many of her songs derive from experiences she had on the road, including impressions of the places she visited, reflections on life as a traveling musician, and portraits of the people she encountered, including those with whom she formed relationships. The latter are generally clear-eyed and unsentimental but can also be romantic ("My Old Man"), exuberant and celebratory ("Carey"), or more distanced and self-examining ("Coyote").

Mitchell studied art and has maintained a parallel career as an exhibiting painter. In both art and music, she takes a particular interest in self-portraiture. Many of the covers of her albums feature painted self-portraits that chronicle her life. Mitchell has said, "My music is not designed to grab instantly. It's designed to wear for a lifetime, to hold up like a fine cloth." She takes this approach to her own music by revisiting her earlier compositions periodically and reworking them in light of her current musical interests. On the 1970 studio version of "Woodstock," Mitchell's paean to the utopian impulses behind the famous rock festival she did not attend, her use of the electric piano gives the song a shimmer that enhances the ethereal and spiritual dimensions of Aquarian lyrics, as do the gospel-inflected backing vocals. In the 1974 live version Mitchell recorded with the jazz-fusion saxophonist Tom Scott and his group the LA Express, the song becomes a funk workout in which the lyrics seem more to be in service to the music than meaningful in themselves. For a subsequent 1980 live version recorded with illustrious contemporary jazz musicians, Mitchell completely alters her phrasing to make the song darker and nostalgic for a time when the sentiments it expresses were current. Finally, in the version on *Travelogue*, the contrast between the stately orchestral setting and Mitchell's somewhat wistful vocal performance makes the song simultaneously cinematic and personal, dramatizing the story of two strangers meeting on a road. Like that piece of fine cloth, Mitchell's music continues to unfold, revealing new patterns with every turn.

QUEEN OF ALT-ROCK
ALANIS MORISSETTE

In 2022, Alanis Morissette released *The Storm Before the Calm*, an album of primarily instrumental ambient meditation music. For those who know Morissette for *Jagged Little Pill*, the 1995 alternative rock album that made her an international star, the contrast is stark. This is not the first time Morissette has knowingly taken a turn in her music that flies in the face of expectation. Morissette, born in Ottawa, Canada, had performed on a television program for children before embracing music. As a teenager, she released two albums of sample-heavy pop dance music. The first, *Alanis* (1991), sold well in Canada,

where Morissette was perceived as a rising star. The second, *Now Is the Time* (1992), did not fare as well, prompting Morissette to move to Los Angeles in search of new musical horizons. The result was *Jagged Little Pill*, a deeply personal album that exposed the psychic wounds of a relationship Morissette had had with an older man, apparently a music business executive.

The anger that fueled this album is palpable from the first song, "All I Really Want," in which Morissette's voice cracks and leaps across registers in a strained tone that sounds scarcely under control. Morissette sings "You Ought to Know" in a breathy,

trembling voice that suggests barely contained rage at the man who betrayed her. As the song gathers momentum, her voice turns into an accusing scream. The lyrics, taken directly from entries in Morissette's diary, a songwriting practice to which she has turned throughout her career, are shockingly intimate. Morissette acknowledges the risk inherent in drawing on her own raw emotions and reactions in her songwriting, remarking, "It's such a fine line between horrifying and unique and rare and special so I'm wire-walking all the time. But what are ya gonna do? These songs are basically diary entries and conversational, that's how it is."

144 Alanis Morissette performs in Hollywood in 1995, the year her breakthrough album *Jagged Little Pill* was released.

145 Alanis Morissette performs in Atlanta in 1996.

For Morissette, the personal is always the political. She sees these songs as responding not just to her treatment at the hands of a specific individual and industry but also to society's treatment of women generally: "I was responding to the patriarchy and my anger and frustration and my eyes rolling." As journalist and cultural critic Rachel Syme points out, Morissette's overt expression of female fury came at the right cultural moment, as women in grunge rock and the riot grrrl movement were communicating similar feelings through music that was much more aggressive and dissonant. Morissette provided a more accessible musical expression of women's sense of crisis. As Syme puts it, riot grrrl and Morissette represent different expressions of women's desire for change: "one was like being at a protest, and the other is like being in therapy." In Morissette's subsequent albums, she continues the project of coming to terms with her trauma and making peace with herself. The song "Hands Clean" (2002) takes another look at the relationship that inspired "You Ought to Know" in a straightforward pop rock style. The song looks at what happened from both her own perspective and that of the other person. Whereas the earlier song conveyed immediate, raw emotion, the later one places the event in the past and is directed less at the object of her rancor than at her own act of addressing it. In "Thank U" (1998), the protagonist thanks both the positive and negative things she has experienced for enabling her to come to terms with her past and herself. In the music video, Morissette appears as a placid naked figure in a city surrounded by people rushing past her without seeing her. Looking at this depiction of a self-contained meditative state, *The Storm Before the Calm* seems more like a chapter in Morissette's ongoing quest for inner peace than a deviation from it.

146 Alanis Morissette performs in the Netherlands in 2005.

147 Alanis Morissette performs in Las Vegas in 2008 as part of her Flavors of Entanglement tour.

FEMME FATALE

NICO

Nico's frequent musical collaborator, multi-instrumentalist and producer John Cale, once said that her music is better understood as belonging to the western classical tradition than as popular, let alone rock, music. Although she always operated within the context of popular music, beginning with her earliest manifestation as a folky pop singer in the Swinging London of 1965, her music is idiosyncratic, experimental, and demanding in ways that link it with art music. Her voice, a deep, stentorian, very clear and clean contralto, was often stereotyped as monotonous and "Teutonic" (presumably because of her German accent) during her brief tenure with that

edgiest of rock bands, the Velvet Underground. When heard to advantage in musical contexts of her own creation, however, her voice is stately and declarative.

When Nico (born Christa Päffgen in Cologne, Germany) surfaced in New York City in 1966, she contacted the artist Andy Warhol, whom she had encountered in London. Previously, she had worked as a model in both Berlin and Paris and appeared in several European films, including Fellini's *La Dolce Vita*. Warhol liked the idea of a beautiful woman fronting the grungy Velvet Underground, whom he managed, and persuaded the group's members to work with

her. She performed with them and sang lead on three tracks of their first album, *The Velvet Underground and Nico*, before embarking on her own musical career. Her first album, *Chelsea Girl* (1967), a reference to the 1966 Warhol film *Chelsea Girls*, in which she had appeared, found her performing in a folk-rock vein. On much of this album, which Nico later disavowed, her voice and the lush instrumentation of guitars, strings, and flutes sound as if they belong to two different musical worlds. Nico's next three albums, *The Marble Index* (1969), *Desertshore* (1970), and *The End* (1974), would reveal a musical vision truly her own. Nico started writing her own songs, with

> Nico in London at the time of the release of her first single in August 1965.

lyrics describing bleak and blasted emotional landscapes sometimes peopled with mythic figures. She also discovered the harmonium, an instrument that provides a drone-like accompaniment well-suited to her propensity for sustained tones. Rather than seeming alien to its setting, Nico's voice blends texturally with the harmonium to produce multi-layered harmonies. There is an element of folk music in this, but not of Greenwich Village. The effect recalls older strains of folk lamentation, particularly traditional Irish forms such as Caoineadh. There are also times on these recordings when Nico's distinctive voice stands on its own, sometimes alternating with instrumental passages. In the haunting "My Only Child," Nico's voice appears solo and against itself as a multi-tracked madrigal choir. In her hands, the Doors' apocalyptic "The End," on which Nico is accompanied primarily by piano and a swirling, menacing pipe organ, becomes something like a German lied. Traditional rock instrumentation kicks in only near the end, to provide a glimpse of hope in the darkness, only to be overtaken by the organ. Nico courted controversy and goaded her audiences. She recorded "Das Lied der Deutschen," the German national anthem better known as "Deutschland Über Alles," originally composed by Haydn, for *The End*. She included the first two verses, which had been removed after the Second World War because of their associations with Nazism. This guaranteed a negative reaction when Nico performed it at concerts in the UK and Europe. She also dedicated the song to Andreas Baader and Ulrike Meinhof, the notorious German far-left terrorists. Exactly what Nico may have meant by this gesture or what the song signified to her as someone who had lived through the war in Germany as a child is impossible to know. The version on the album, in which Nico accompanies herself on the harmonium, is dissonant and haunted, hardly a stirring assertion of national identity.

Nico's music was outside the mainstream by her own choice and consequently underappreciated in her lifetime, though she was celebrated and befriended by Siouxsie Sioux, Patti Smith, and John Lydon (Johnny Rotten) and has been called the first goth rocker. Recent years have seen renewed interest in Nico, who died in 1988, as well as a reevaluation of her music and acknowledgment of its importance and influence.

150–151 A 1966 photo shoot at Andy Warhol's studio the Factory. From left: John Cale, Gerard Malanga, Nico, Warhol.

THE ANTI-POP STAR
SINÉAD O'CONNOR

<Sinéad O'Connor performs in the Netherlands, 1988.

In 1992, Sinéad O'Connor appeared on the US television program *Saturday Night Live*. For her second song, O'Connor sang an a cappella version of Bob Marley's "War." When she arrived at a lyric about the conflict between good and evil, she held up a photo of Pope John Paul II and tore it up, saying, "Fight the real enemy." This was intended to protest the Catholic Church's silence on child abuse. O'Connor had been raised Irish Catholic, and the photo was one she had taken from her mother's house upon her death, giving the gesture a deeply personal meaning. It was perceived, however, as O'Connor's committing professional suicide by turning her back on the success she had achieved with her international #1 hit of 1990, a powerfully emotive reading of Prince's "Nothing Compares 2 U," equal parts anger and loneliness at the departure of a lover, and two well-received albums.

Although O'Connor was on her way to becoming a major international pop star, this was not what she wanted. "An artist's job is sometimes to create difficult conversations that need to be had," she has said. "That's what art is for." The world of pop music did not provide her with a platform for the uncompromising personal expression in which she engages, in both music and politics. When a record executive told her to let her hair grow out to appear more feminine, she shaved her head instead. Her appearance thus became a statement against the effort to constrain women to normative social standards, just as her music is a no-holds-barred expression of raw emotion and political rage. Subsequent revelations about the church's silence on child abuse and the #MeToo movement's exposure of the mistreatment of women in the entertainment business show that in the early 1990s, O'Connor was already drawing attention to issues that would only receive wide attention decades later. In July 2023, Sinéad O'Connor died in London at the age of just 56.

QUEEN OF COUNTRY
DOLLY PARTON

When Dolly Parton was offered membership in the Rock and Roll Hall of Fame in 2022, she initially turned down the honor on the grounds that she is a country artist, not a rocker. Ultimately, she relented, took up an electric guitar, and performed at the induction ceremony a new song about her love for the rock and roll with which she grew up in the 1950s and its influence on her as a country musician. In fact, Parton is no stranger to rock, pop, and even funk, having recorded versions of songs ranging from Sly and the Family Stone's "Everyday People" to Led Zeppelin's

"Stairway to Heaven." In her own music, Parton has ventured beyond the confines of country many times, notably from 1977 to 1982 when she strove, successfully, for pop stardom but lost her die-hard country fans. She reasserted her deep country roots with her first bluegrass album, *The Grass Is Blue* (1999).

Raised in poverty in Appalachia, Parton saw music as her way out of a rural life that offered her no prospects. "I wanted to be free," she has said. "I had my songs to sing. I had an ambition and it burned inside me. It was something I knew would take me out of

the mountains. I knew I could see worlds beyond the Smoky Mountains." Many of Parton's songs look back on her origins without nostalgia and detail the hard life and social stigma of being poor. Many others, including "9 to 5," about working women, and "An Eagle When She Flies," specifically speak to women's lives and celebrate their strength. Her stage persona is intentionally hyper-feminine to a degree that parodies the stereotype of women in country music, thus undermining the stereotype. Her 1967 song "Dumb Blonde" says it all: underestimate a woman at your own peril.

MILITANT PUNK-FEMINIST STREET BAND

PUSSY RIOT

< Anonymous members of Pussy Riot perform at the 2017 Day for Night festival of music and visual art in Houston.

The performances of Pussy Riot, the self-described Russian "militant punk-feminist street band," are equal parts punk rock, political protest, and performance art. The group formed in Moscow in 2011, after Vladimir Putin declared his intention to run for a third term as president, to protest what they call the "Putinist junta." It is a collective of variable personnel whose ten to twenty members perform in colorful but interchangeable dresses and balaclavas to hide their identities. Despite these attempts at anonymity, they regularly have been subject to harassment, arrest, and imprisonment.

Although Pussy Riot sometimes plays conventional music venues, including the Glastonbury Festival in 2015 and with Madonna at an Amnesty International benefit concert in the United States, they are committed to performing illegally at public sites in Russia. Such sites have included a Moscow subway platform, Red Square, a boutique shopping district, and outside a prison. The event that brought them the most notoriety took place on February 21, 2012, when members of Pussy Riot invaded the Cathedral of Christ the Savior in Moscow. Four colorfully dressed

women with balaclavas covering their faces danced and jumped around making punching motions while shouting their "punk prayer," "Mother of God, Drive Putin Away," a diatribe against the Russian Orthodox Church's sexism and support of Putin and the KGB.

After being removed quickly by security, three alleged members of the group were arrested, put on trial for hooliganism, and sentenced to two years in prison. Although Yekaterina Samutsevich was given a suspended sentence, Nadezhda Tolokonnikova and Maria Alyokhina were incarcerated.

158 Yekaterina Samutsevich, Maria Alyokhina, and Nadezhda Tolokonnikova confined to a glass cage while on trial in Moscow in August 2012 following their arrest for Pussy Riot's guerilla performance at the Cathedral of Christ the Savior six months earlier.

The fourth participant, Diana Burkot, was not caught and went into hiding. Tolokonnikova's and Alyokhina's sentences prompted protests on the parts of international artists and human rights activists. At Christmas 2013, the two women were released under amnesty. Over time, they have largely abandoned anonymity to become the most visible faces of Pussy Riot, expressing their political and social views through music videos and live performances. Less than two months after their release, members of Pussy Riot filmed the video for their song "Putin Will Teach You to Love the Motherland" in Sochi, during the 2014 Winter Olympics. They disrupted another high-profile sporting event, the 2018 World Cup in Moscow, by running out onto the pitch dressed as police officers.

Pussy Riot has expanded the scope of their activism beyond Russia. In 2014, they collaborated with members of other groups on a video made in New York City for the song "I Can't Breathe," the last words of Eric Garner, an African American victim of police brutality, their first song in English. In the video, Tolokonnikova and Alyokhina are buried alive wearing Russian riot police

159 Nadezhda Tolokonnikova, also known as Nadya Riot, hosting a digital art event at the Superchief Gallery in Los Angeles during NFT Week in April 2022.

uniforms. As dirt is thrown into their faces, the song's lyrics speak of darkness and death against a steady drumbeat. When they are fully buried, the voice of punk legend Richard Hell is heard speaking the last things Garner said to the police before he died.

On February 20, 2022, almost ten years to the day after Pussy Riot's demonstration at the cathedral, Putin ordered the Russian invasion of Ukraine. In the crackdown against dissent that followed, people associated with Pussy Riot were continually arrested and incarcerated for protesting the war. Alyokhina was sentenced to twenty-one days in a penal colony. Despite their commitment to an ongoing critique of the Russian government, several members of Pussy Riot, including Alyokhina and Burkot, fled Russia to live in exile. In the spring of 2022, Pussy Riot launched a tour in Berlin with stops throughout Europe and in the United States to benefit Ukrainian war victims.

GLAM ROCKER

SUZI QUATRO

< Suzi Quatro brings the noise at the Hammersmith Odeon, London, 1978.

When Suzi Quatro appeared as a guest on the British music television program *Gas Tank* in 1983, she pointedly asked whether she was "the only female who has ever been on this show." Keyboardist Rick Wakeman, the host, demurred and offered the name of a singer, to which Quatro responded, "She didn't play an instrument." When Quatro had first made a name for herself some ten years earlier, she was the only woman fronting a rock band not just as a singer but also as a songwriter, group leader, and bass guitarist. Because she served as a role model for a generation of hard-rocking women, the

word *iconic* frequently appears next to her name. Among the many women musicians who have claimed her as an inspiration are the Runaways, Joan Jett, Tina Weymouth of Talking Heads, Chrissie Hynde of the Pretenders, and the British metal band Girlschool.

From a very early age, Quatro, who was born into a musical family and grew up in a suburb of Detroit, sat in with her father's jazz band, the Art Quatro Trio, as a percussionist. Inspired by seeing the Beatles on television, her older sister Patti Quatro (later a guitarist in the pioneering all-woman rock band Fanny) started a female

garage band called the Pleasure Seekers. Suzi, then fourteen years old, joined the quintet as bassist and occasional singer. The Pleasure Seekers were mainstays on the Detroit-area music scene, rubbing shoulders with the likes of the MC5, the Stooges, and Alice Cooper. In 1967, they played for wounded American troops at an army hospital in Vietnam. By 1969, the group had become the more hippie-oriented Cradle, and it was with this group that Quatro was spotted in 1971 by the British record producer Mickie Most, who offered to work with her on the condition that she move to England.

161

162 Suzi Quatro rocks the Electric Ballroom in Atlanta with her band in 1974.

163 Suzi Quatro in full glam regalia.

Quatro's career in the United Kingdom got off to an uncertain start until Most introduced her to Mike Chapman and Nicky Chinn, the songwriting and production team known collectively as Chinnichap. Quatro joined their roster of commercially successful glam rock acts that included Sweet and Mud. The first Chinnichap song she released as a single, "Can the Can," reached #1 on the charts in the spring of 1973, a feat she repeated in the fall of 1974 with "Devil Gate Drive." Between 1973 and 1979, Quatro charted twelve times.

Quatro's performance persona is as important as her musical prowess. She describes herself as "a rocker from the Elvis, Little Richard school," an identity for which there were no female role models. Quatro used the gender ambiguity that was at the heart of glam rock to her advantage; it allowed her to craft the defining image of the woman rock and roller. Whereas most glam artists were men who dressed and made up flamboyantly, Quatro wore a black leather jumpsuit and little makeup. She performed songs like the Beatles' "I Wanna Be Your Man" without changing the gendered pronouns, placing herself in the masculine position and implying that the object of her affection is female. Although diminutive in size, Quatro is a dominant figure onstage. She is in constant motion, bass guitar slung low on her right hip, bobbing and stomping to the beat, shaking her head, pumping her fists. Her onstage persona became the basis for Leather Tuscadero, the character she played on the US television program *Happy Days* in 1977–78.

Now in her early seventies, Quatro has been performing and recording nonstop for nearly sixty years. Ever the quintessential rocker, she has more than accomplished the mission she set for herself of "kicking down the male door in rock and roll and proving that a female MUSICIAN...could play as well if not better than the boys."

BLUES WOMAN

BONNIE RAITT

Bonnie Raitt is many things: singer, songwriter, political activist, veteran of the early '70s Laurel Canyon music scene in Los Angeles. She is also one of only two women on the *Rolling Stone* list of the 100 Greatest Guitarists (the other is Joni Mitchell). She is particularly lauded for playing slide guitar, a technique she taught herself as a teenager inspired by blues legend Robert Johnson's recordings. Because she had only heard and never seen a slide guitar player, she put her bottleneck slide on her middle finger rather than the usual ring finger. By the time Raitt realized her mistake, she was too settled in her approach to change it.

Although she originally played acoustic slide guitar, she is best-known for playing slide on an electric Fender Stratocaster. In 1967, Raitt was a college student in Cambridge, Massachusetts, when she decided to pursue music and began hanging out at local clubs. She met and performed with many of her blues idols and became a tireless advocate for musicians of earlier generations, including Mississippi Fred McDowell and singer Sippie Wallace. She has recorded their songs, insisted they be hired as her opening acts, and shared television appearances with them.

Like many musicians steeped in the blues, Raitt's singing is in

dialogue with her guitar. As Paul Elie has written in *The New Yorker*, "For Raitt, slide is a second voice, much like her first: tough, physical, subtle, and frankly emotional." This second voice has evolved over time. Whereas Raitt's earlier slide playing was very much in the traditional blues style represented by McDowell, she has found ways of incorporating the technique into songs with a loping jazz cadence. In this context, the slide is less a means of finding microtonal blue notes and more a way of articulating sustained, lyrical passages that sometimes hint at the style's origins in Hawaiian slack-key guitar.

> Bonnie Raitt and her Fender Stratocaster, the guitar with which she is most identified.

COUNTRY ROCK PIONEER
LINDA RONSTADT

< Portrait of Linda Ronstadt, c. 1980.

Lauded as one of the greatest interpretive singers in popular music, Linda Ronstadt was raised on the ranch of a prosperous family of combined German and Mexican heritage in Tucson, Arizona. Ronstadt grew up surrounded by country music and Mexican music. These, and many other styles and genres, would permeate her own music.

At the age of eighteen, Ronstadt headed for Los Angeles, where she helped form the Stone Poneys. Although the group was a folk-rock trio, their one hit, "Different Drum" (1967), was arranged as baroque pop, showcasing the versatility and purity of tone that would define Ronstadt's career as a singer.

Ronstadt's early career as a solo artist saw her move across genres. She performed at folk clubs in Los Angeles and New York, yet her debut album, *Hand Sown…Home Grown* (1969), has been called the first alternative country album by a female artist. She was equally likely to be interviewed in the pages of *Rolling Stone* as in those of *Country-Western Stars*. After struggling to balance her interests in folk, country, rock, and pop, she forged a stylistic synthesis that allowed her to perform songs from a range of genres in a way that was recognizably her own. Although many of her best-known songs were country-flavored, her biggest hit, "You're

No Good" (1974), originated as a soul number. From 1974 through 1980, Ronstadt produced five hit albums and was the biggest female rock singer on the arena circuit. Feeling that she had established herself as an artist, Ronstadt moved in other directions in the 1980s that included operetta; Spanish-language explorations of her Mexican heritage, beginning with *Canciones de Mi Padre* (1987); and jazz and pop standards. She returned to a purer country sound together with Dolly Parton and Emmylou Harris as the Trio. Ronstadt retired from singing in 2013 after being diagnosed with a degenerative muscle disease.

MISS ROSS

DIANA ROSS

< Photo of Diana Ross in Los Angeles, 1987, by Harry Langdon, the photographer who has produced many of her iconic images.

Diana Ross's story is inextricable from that of the Supremes, the girl group she founded in 1959 with three friends she had grown up with in segregated public housing in Detroit. Initially called the Primettes, the four teenagers won an audition at Motown Records in a talent contest and signed a contract as the Supremes in 1961. Whereas the Primettes had been a female doo wop group with an ensemble sound, the Supremes were built around Ross's warm, clarion lyric soprano and her vivacious onstage personality. Although the Supremes dressed in identical high-fashion gowns and engaged in unison choreography, their

staging set Ross apart from the others. In 1964, the Supremes had an extraordinary run of five #1 pop hits beginning with "Where Did Our Love Go?" Ross's meteoric rise would be symbiotically linked with that of her group and its label until she left the Supremes in 1970.

Although Motown employed almost exclusively Black artists, the vision of founder Berry Gordy Jr. was to forge a style from the R&B and vocal harmony music made for Black audiences since the 1940s that would appeal to all audiences. Nevertheless, the ambassadors of this music were Black musicians at a complicated moment in

the history of race relations in the United States. By 1964, the civil rights movement had achieved some success, but hostile attitudes toward Black people persisted. The glamour, refinement, and good humor Ross and the Supremes brought to their public personae countered prevailing racist stereotypes and made them important role models for young Black women. The fact that three Black women were perceived as fashion icons was socially significant. The group also served as a template for subsequent Black girl groups, including Destiny's Child, En Vogue, and TLC.

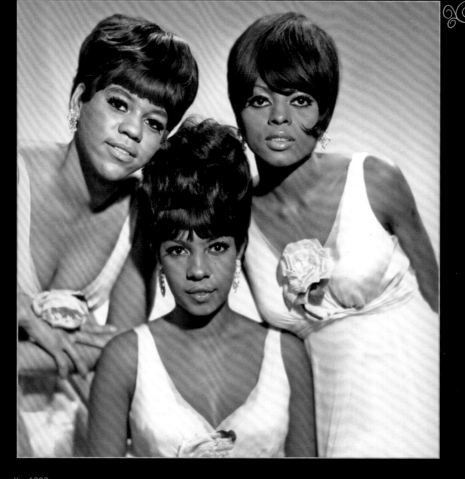

170 Photo of Diana Ross from the 1960s.

171 The classic lineup of the Supremes. From left: Florence Ballard, Mary Wilson, and Diana Ross.

Wanting to be perceived as mainstream entertainers, Ross and the Supremes recorded a wide variety of material, including thematic albums devoted to the Liverpool sound, country music, Christmas music, show tunes, and the music of Sam Cooke. Although topical songs were not a big part of the Supremes' repertoire, they recorded Cooke's "A Change Is Gonna Come." Two of their 1968 hits touch on social issues: "Love Child" addresses the stigma associated with children born out of wedlock, while "I'm Living in Shame" deals with class distinctions. Ross and the group moved with the times, adopting mod fashion and incorporating elements of psychedelic rock into their music on "Reflections" (1968) and Ross's funky solo version of the Beatles' "Come Together" (1970).

In the jacket photo for *Diana Ross* (1970), her first solo album, a dressed-down Ross is depicted as a skinny waif with close-cropped hair and big, hopeful eyes. This did not represent Ross's abandonment of chic—she even appeared at the 2022 Glastonbury Festival in a sequined gown and bouffant hair—but it did draw a clear line between her former identity as a Supreme and her new identity as a solo artist. This album gave Ross her first big hit with her smoldering version of "Ain't No Mountain High Enough" and one of her signature songs, "Reach Out and Touch (Somebody's Hand)." She repeated this feat in 1980 with *Diana*, again with a casual image on the jacket and two striking performances, the disco-influenced "Upside Down" and "I'm Coming Out." As she approaches eighty years old, Ross continues to perform regularly, including residencies in Las Vegas, home of the entertainment world glamour she has

172 Diana Ross performs at Wembley Arena, London, in 2004.

173 Diana Ross performs a medley of her solo hits.

QUEEN OF LATIN MUSIC
SHAKIRA

> Photo of Shakira in 2002.

Shakira Isabel Mebarak Ripoll, born in Colombia to a Lebanese father and a Colombian mother, hit her stride when her 1995 album *Pies Descalzos (Barefoot)* catapulted her into the world-wide Spanish-language music market. The Cuban American Latin music luminary Gloria Estefan, seeing in Shakira the potential to be a major pop artist, helped her expand her audience further by translating some of her lyrics into English. Shakira learned to speak the language herself, took over the task of translating her own songs, and began writing directly in English. She released her first English-language album, *Laundry Service*, in 2001, which yielded the infectious international Top 10 hit "Whenever, Wherever." An established star for over two decades, Shakira has crossed back and forth between the Spanish- and English-language markets, earning international awards and plaudits along the way.

To describe Shakira in terms of crossover, however, does not do justice to the range of music she synthesizes to create distinctive hybrid styles. It is significant that in 2000, Shakira won the Latin Grammys for both Female Pop Vocal Performance and Female

176 Shakira performing on German television in 2005.

177 Shakira performing in Mexico City on her Oral Fixation tour, 2006.

178–179 Shakira performing "Waka Waka (This Time for Africa)," the official song of the 2010 World Cup in South Africa.

Rock Vocal Performance for two different songs, suggesting her ability to work in different genres of music. Her concerts range freely over a myriad of styles that includes rock, pop, piano ballads, Latin pop, reggaeton, and Middle Eastern–influenced dance pop. In many of Shakira's songs, she juxtaposes different genres, including a wide range of Latin styles and their respective instrumentation. "Objection (Tango)" (2002) begins with traditional Argentinian tango instruments—piano, double bass, and bandoneon. Rock instrumentation kicks in at the verse, including an Eddie Cochran–style rock and roll guitar. "Whenever, Wherever" partakes of a similar synthesis, albeit with different cultural referents. The song opens with reverb-heavy electric rock guitar that quickly gives way to Andean instrumentation that includes the bombo leguero, charango, quena flute, and pan pipes. A wordless refrain that hints at an Arabic scale is underpinned by surf guitar.

Shakira celebrates her Lebanese heritage by incorporating Arabic scales and instruments into her music and occasionally by singing in Arabic. Two of her given names are Arabic: Shakira, meaning "thankful," and Mebarak, meaning "blessed." She describes herself by saying, "I am a fusion. That's my persona. I'm a fusion between black and white, between pop and rock, between cultures—between my Lebanese father and my mother's Spanish blood, the Colombian folklore and Arab dance."

"Ojos Así" (1998), whose lyrics are in Spanish, is explicitly an Arab pop song with combined Middle Eastern and rock instrumentation. Shakira's style of dancing in her videos and live performances combines Middle Eastern belly dancing, which she started learning as a child, with Afro-Colombian folk dances. Shakira brings disparate cultures together not only to foreground her own hybrid identity but also to create bridges between them through musical sound. Shakira's performance of "Whenever, Wherever" at a 2007 concert in Dubai included an extended passage of belly dancing accompanied by music in microtonal Arabic scales played on two different instruments: the qanun, an Arabic zither, and an electric lap steel guitar, an instrument associated with blues, rock, and country music. That the scalar characteristics of Arab music can be achieved using either instrument reveals a sonic common ground. Something similar happens in "Objection (Tango)" when the syncopated rhythm and the bandoneon's accordion-like sound are reminiscent of Cajun dance music. Shakira uses her platform and syncretic approach to draw attention to under-recognized cultures. For her Superbowl performance in 2020, Shakira included two dances from the Afro-Colombian community, descendants of slaves brought to Colombia as laborers, mapalé and champeta. A video of Shakira learning champeta from Liz Dany Campo Diaz, from Shakira's hometown, went viral and initiated an online "champeta challenge" for which thousands of people posted videos of themselves performing the dance.

180 Shakira performs at Rock in Rio, Madrid, Spain, 2008.

181 Shakira performs on Spanish television to promote her new album, *Servicio de Lavandería (Laundry Service)*, in 2001.

182–183 Shakira performs on the opening night of the Tour of the Mongoose in Barcelona, on December 10, 2022.

HIGH PRIESTESS OF PUNK

SIOUXSIE SIOUX

In 1987, Siouxsie and the Banshees recorded a version of Iggy Pop's "The Passenger." Four years earlier, they had produced a respectful version of the Beatles' "Dear Prudence," replete with psychedelic phasing effects, a #3 hit in the UK. Paying homage to Pop, often considered to be "the Godfather of Punk," is something a group that had emerged in 1976 from the London punk scene might be expected to do. Recording a Beatles song, on the other hand, runs counter to the anti-art, anti-mainstream ideology of punk. This underlines the point that while Siouxsie and the Banshees formed in the context of punk, the context did not define them. Frontwoman Siouxsie Sioux (born Susan Janet Ballion) took the DIY ethic of punk to heart, interpreting it to mean that she had the freedom to assert a unique musical identity that overlapped punk and anticipated goth without belonging to either.

Although Siouxsie and the Banshees gathered a following in the mid-1970s by playing in clubs and Sioux gained publicity as a fashion-forward face of punk, the group struggled to get a record contract. She attributed this difficulty to their "morbid sense of humor" and to the music industry's inability to take women seriously. "If it's a girl, 'Oh, she's just flogging an image, she hasn't got anything to say.' They like that. Whereas if they think she's got as much there as anyone else, and more so, they don't like it."

The group's first album, *The Scream* (1978), partakes of punk anomie and aggression, though the music is quite different from punk in style. It is as intense as punk, but sparer—each instrument is clearly defined as a distinct voice. It is rhythmically precise—much of its impact comes from the interplay of Sioux's percussive vocals with the insistent pounding of the rhythm section. The songs are

> Siouxsie Sioux performs with Siouxsie and the Banshees at the Rainbow Theatre in London in 1978.

in minor keys and are dark in perspective. "Mirage" is a scathing critique of the artificiality of images purveyed by the media. "Jigsaw Feeling" describes a fragmented psyche, while "Suburban Relapse" depicts a disaffected housewife's descent into homicidal rage. "Switch" is a frightening six-minute dramatic diatribe on the power of scientists, physicians, and clergy over people's lives.

On this album, Sioux sings in her lower range in a thunderous voice that becomes like a chant in places. Her emphasis on vocal power and presence over melody distances her from the audience and defines a compelling but unapproachable persona. As a band, Siouxsie and the Banshees lasted over twenty years. In that time, it became clear that Sioux is a versatile performer able both to sing playfully in a lighter soprano (as on "Dear Prudence") and to delve into the darker recesses of the human experience. Many of their more up-tempo songs are dance club favorites, even when the lyrics are ominous. The surface cheeriness of "Happy House" belies its sardonic take on suburban living in which everyone pretends all is well. "Red Light," a denunciation of the way women are objectified, incorporates elements of electronic dance music.

Rhythm, always the Banshees' secret weapon, became the main focus of the Creatures, centered on a duo of Sioux and the Banshees' drummer, Budgie. The Creatures' music is built around multi-layered percussion tracks, some sampled, and Sioux's voice, sometimes multi-tracked, and punctuated with a variety of instrumental sounds. This group's first EP included a version of the rock standard "Wild Thing," almost unrecognizable save for the lyrics, performed with keening vocals and tribal-sounding percussion. Sioux released her only solo album, *Mantaray*, in 2007. She has performed and recorded sporadically since. In 2022, it was announced that Sioux will perform live for the first time in ten years at the 2023 Latitude Festival.

186 Photo of Siouxsie and the Banshees, 1979. From left: guitarist John McKay, singer Siouxsie Sioux, bassist Steven Severin, and drummer Kenny Morris.

187 Studio shot of Siouxsie Sioux, London, 1979.

POLITICAL ROCKER

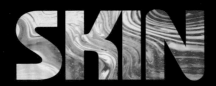
SKIN

Skin (Deborah Anne Dyer) is the singer and frontwoman of Skunk Anansie, a multi-racial British rock band named for an animal that is both black and white and a West Indian trickster spider god who is a symbol of resistance to oppression. The group is known for songs that articulate Skin's political and social views in very direct terms. "Skunk Anansie are political because I'm from Brixton," she has said, referring to an area of London where many West Indian immigrants, including her Jamaican parents, settled. The Brixton riots of 1981 and 1985, both sparked by the treatment of the area's Black population at the hands

of the police, were formative experiences for Skin. Skunk Anansie's "And Here I Stand," from their first album, *Paranoid and Sunburnt* (1995), vividly describes anger at a lack of recognition that spills over into violence. The band's heavy metal sound, inspired by American grunge rock, provides Skin the means to express the rage she feels at the racism, sexism, and homophobia she experiences as a queer, British-born Black woman. One of Skin's muses is Nina Simone. She notes that whereas Simone's music was intensely political, she wrote about how social circumstances made her feel and did not claim to speak for a collective identity.

Although Skin addresses systemic issues in her songs, she does so from an individual perspective rooted in her own experiences and encounters.

Skin is critical of the marginalization of women and Black people in rock culture, feeling that Skunk Anansie was not perceived as a legitimate rock band in the 1990s because it has two Black members. She further argues that "Black women from Tina Turner to Grace Jones and Mel B are perceived as aggressive, overtly sexual, animalistic, panthers in cages," and that they are expected to embody this stereotype. "The industry then was owned and run by middle-

190 Skin sings with Skunk Anansie at the Brixton Academy, London, in 2009.

191 The members of Skunk Anansie in 1998. From left to right: guitarist Ace (Martin Kent), lead singer Skin (Deborah Anne Dyer), Mark Richardson (drums), and bassist Cass (Richard Lewis).

aged white men. If you weren't sexual they didn't know what to do with you. You made them feel uncomfortable, because you weren't playing the game." Nevertheless, Skunk Anansie made it to the UK Top 20 six times between 1996 and 1999 and gained enough acclaim to be invited to headline the 1999 Glastonbury Festival, making Skin the event's first Black British headliner.

Not all of Skin's songs for Skunk Anansie are political: many concern the emotions resulting from agonizing moments in relationships, which Skin approaches with the same anger and sense of betrayal she brings to her socially oriented music. The protagonist of "Secretly," a song that shows the range of styles Skunk Anansie employs beyond hard rock and the precision and versatility of Skin's singing, is trying mightily to maintain her cool while talking with a friend she secretly lusts after. The song begins with orchestral strings leading into an electronic pulse, then spare guitar and drums as Skin enters, singing in a hushed yet urgent tone about the discomfort of trying to maintain a façade of objectivity. Skin builds emotional tension by moving into her rock timbre. As the orchestra returns, Skin moves to a wide-open power ballad voice that brings this section of the song to a climax. As she returns to her more restrained style of singing, the stylistic cycle begins again to indicate the frustration and lack of resolution the song describes.

Skunk Anansie disbanded in 2001 for what proved to be a nine-year hiatus, successfully reconvening in 2009. During this time, Skin produced two solo albums, *Fleshwounds* (2003) and *Fake Chemical State* (2008). The former was a departure for Skin, an album of meditative ballads on relationships in a keyboard-driven R&B style for which Skin sings in a husky soprano. The latter is a rock album that opens with the rousing punk of "Alone in My Room" and ventures into mainstream rock and even new wave on "Purple."

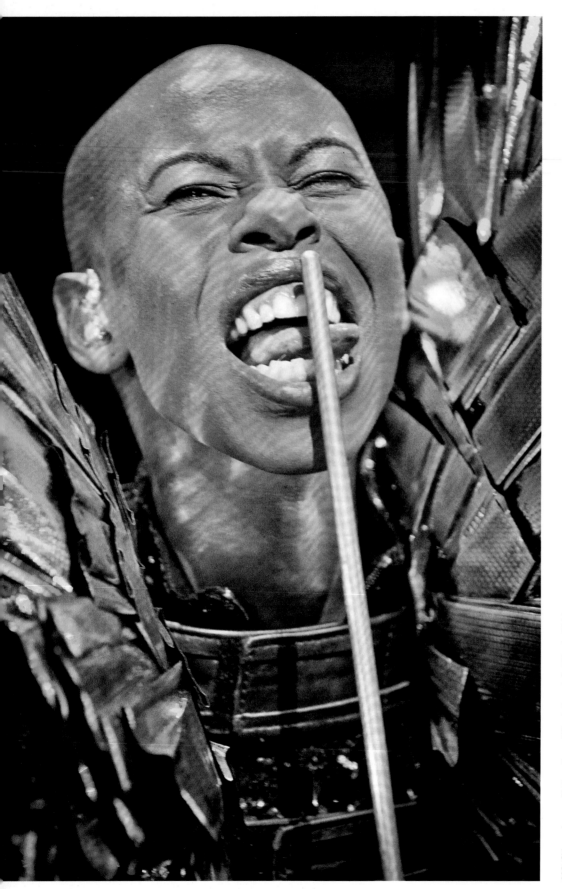
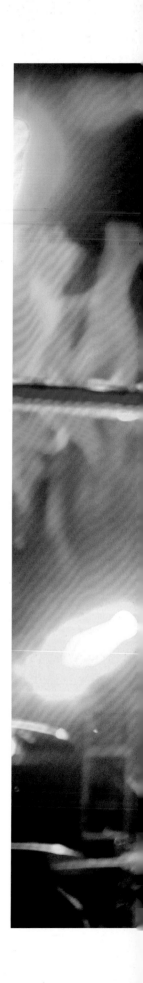

192 Skin performs with the reformed Skunk Anansie in Milan in 2011.

193 Skin performs with Skunk Anansie at the Schengenfest 2013 music festival in Vinica, Slovenia.

194–195 Skin crowd surfs while performing with Skunk Anansie in Milan in 2016.

COUNTERCULTURAL GODDESS
GRACE SLICK

< Grace Slick's compelling presence and powerful singing voice made her a mainstay of psychedelic rock.

Stephen Stills's song "Rock & Roll Woman," recorded by Buffalo Springfield in 1967, is said to have been inspired by Grace Slick, one of the quintessential rock and roll women of the 1960s. A commanding presence on stage with a powerful singing voice and a dramatic delivery, mercurial and possessed of a rebellious and iconoclastic spirit, Slick was at the epicenter of the youth counterculture in San Francisco.

Slick, born Grace Barnett Wing, grew up largely in San Francisco. After a brief time as a college student in New York and Florida, Slick returned there

and worked as a department store model. In 1965, Slick was inspired by seeing Jefferson Airplane perform to start her own group, the Great Society, with her husband and brother-in-law. With Slick as keyboard player and lead singer, the group contributed to the development of psychedelic rock, particularly by incorporating the influence of classical Indian music, and performed regularly at San Francisco venues such as Jefferson Airplane's home club, the Matrix, and the Fillmore. They were on the verge of signing a recording contract when Slick left to join Jefferson Airplane after founding member

Signe Toly Anderson departed. She brought two songs with her: "Somebody to Love," written by her brother-in-law Darby Slick, and "White Rabbit," which she had composed. Sung by Slick, both were Top 10 hits for the Airplane in 1967.

With Slick on board, Jefferson Airplane developed into an archetypal psychedelic rock band. They became known as the "house band" at the Fillmore and appeared at the era-defining festivals of the 1960s, including the Monterey International Pop Festival in 1967 and Woodstock in 1969. The Airplane's presence on the pop charts allowed them to serve as informal cultural ambassadors representing the San Francisco hippie scene to the rest of the United States. Slick often used the group's media appearances as opportunities for social and political provocation. When the Airplane made an unlikely television appearance on the straightlaced Dick Clark's teen dance program *American Bandstand* in June 1967, where they talked about the upcoming Summer of Love, Slick appeared dressed in a nun's habit. When they appeared on *The Smothers Brothers Comedy Hour* the next year, Slick wore dark makeup and gave a Black Power salute at the end of the performance, explaining later that she did this both to signal solidarity with the African American cause and because she "knew nearly everybody would object to it."

As a vocalist, Slick was inclined to experiment. She often used unconventional phrasing, sustaining tones at length, and emphasizing unexpected parts of the melody and lyrics. She used wordless vocalizations, sometimes aggressively and sometimes very quietly, often shifting her dynamics. She improvised in ways that meant her performances of songs in the Airplane's repertoire were very different from one another. At Woodstock, accompanied only by the group's drummer, she altered a section of the very familiar "Somebody to Love" to celebrate the morning to such a degree that it became a new piece of music.

From 1970 to 1973, Slick was a key participant in the Planet Earth Rock and Roll Orchestra (PERRO), an informal alliance of California musicians that included members of the Grateful Dead, Crosby, Stills and Nash, and Quicksilver Messenger Service. The collective released albums under the names of various artists. The first was Jefferson Starship's *Blows Against the Empire* of 1970, in which Slick was vocally prominent, and Slick's first solo album, *Manhole* (1974), was also a PERRO production. By contrast with Slick's work with rock groups, her solo recordings often place her powerful voice in lush orchestral settings.

By 1972, creative and personal tensions caused Jefferson Airplane to split up. Half of the group, including Slick, continued from 1974 until 1988 as Jefferson Starship, later called Starship, a more pop-oriented group. Insisting that rock music is for the young, Slick retired in 1989, saying, with typical acerbity, "I don't like old people on a rock-and-roll stage. I think they look pathetic, me included." Since then, she has devoted herself to painting, selling her sixties-inspired work through art galleries.

198–199 Grace Slick hangs out onstage with other members of Jefferson Airplane, singer Country Joe McDonald, and rock impresario Bill Graham at the Woodstock Music and Art Fair in 1969.

POET LAUREATE
OF PUNK
PATTI SMITH

Patti Smith's first single, from 1974, has a poem on one side and a staple of garage rock on the other. The poem is "Piss Factory," a profane rant of working-class frustration that incorporates lines from well-known rock songs of the 1960s. Smith is joined by pianist Richard Sohl, whose accompaniment emphasizes the rhythm of her speech. On the other side of the disc, Smith prefaces the rock standard "Hey Joe" with a text addressing the famous photograph of the radicalized heiress Patty Hearst posed holding a rifle in front of the flag of the Symbionese Liberation Army.

From this, Smith moves into the song, taking it at a slow tempo initially, then building in urgency as she abandons the song's lyrics in a seemingly improvised flow around the idea of freedom that circles back to the photograph.

Smith has called herself a poet who "got sidetracked" by music. She has defined her artistic vision by saying, "I wanted to infuse the written word with the immediacy and frontal attack of rock and roll." It would be fair to say that the reverse is also true, that she brought the urgent, personal voice of a beat poet to rock music. Alternately, it might be said that she revealed

the quality of immediacy shared by contemporary poetry and rock and roll. Smith's prosody is earthy and rhythmic. She uses repetition to make vernacular language sound like a mantra or incantation. When performing, she extends words in a manner akin to a sustained tone in music.

A bookish, sickly child who grew up as an outsider in rural New Jersey, Smith moved to New York City in 1967 at the age of twenty. She knew New York primarily through abstract expressionist paintings but believed it to be an environment in which she would be able to express her inner creativity.

Smith became an active participant in the downtown arts scene. In the early 1970s, Smith published several books of poems and was associated with the distinguished Poetry Project at St. Mark's Church in the East Village. Just as beat poets and jazz musicians performed together, Smith asked guitarist Lenny Kaye to accompany her for her first reading at the church in 1971. In the same year, she wrote and performed the play *Cowboy Mouth* with the playwright and actor Sam Shepard. She also made drawings, some of which are in the collection of the Museum of Modern Art in New York.

When Smith first started performing at downtown clubs such as Max's Kansas City and CBGB, she did so as a poet, only to discover that the crowd was more receptive when she was accompanied by Kaye on guitar. Her confrontational style of performing, an amalgamation of concert, spoken word, poetry, and ritual, made her a key figure on the turbulent scene that was the crucible of punk rock and new wave. Smith's first album, *Horses* (1975), formalized the experiments she had conducted at poetry readings and punk clubs, with stripped-down rock music and poetic language pushing each other toward stratospheric heights of urgency and energy. The cover is a photograph of Smith by Robert Mapplethorpe that became an iconic image of androgyny. After Smith's second album, *Radio Ethiopia* (1976), was not well received, she returned with *Easter* (1978), an album with a more conventional rock sound, strong vocal performances, and Smith's best-known song, "Because the Night," which had been left unfinished by Bruce Springsteen and completed by Smith with Springsteen's blessing. An artist whose career now spans six decades, Smith is an internationally admired though never quite mainstream cultural figure. She is a creative spirit for whom self-expression is more important than the medium through which the self is expressed.

202 Guitarist Lenny Kaye (standing) and Patti Smith (lying down) performing in 1976.

203 Patti Smith performing at the Electric Ballroom in Atlanta in 1976.

204–205 Patti Smith performs songs from her *Easter* album during a 1979 concert at the Palladium in Hollywood.

206–207 Patti Smith performs during the 62nd Sanremo Music Festival in 2012.

"To me, punk rock is the freedom to create, freedom to be successful, freedom to not be successful, freedom to be who you are. It's freedom."

—Patti Smith

FROM COUNTRY TO POP
TAYLOR SWIFT

< Taylor Swift performs in Nashville during the tour for *1989*, the album with which she marked her transition from country music to pop in 2015.

210–211 Taylor Swift performs in Los Angeles, 2015, on her 1989 World Tour. The style of the performance underlines her departure from the conventions of country music.

In 2014, Taylor Swift released *1989*, an album titled after the year she was born that marked a musical rebirth. Swift, previously identified with country music, declared *1989* to be her first "official pop album," completing a stylistic transition she had already hinted at with her previous album, *Red* (2012). When Swift was thirteen, her family moved from Pennsylvania to Tennessee to allow her to fulfill her musical ambitions in Nashville, the capital of country music. Initially seeking to make her mark as a songwriter, Swift attracted the attention of the music industry with her performances and had a record

deal by the time she was sixteen. Her first single, and first hit, "Tim McGraw," named for a favorite country artist, is a wistful reflection on summer love presented with full acoustic country instrumentation of guitars and fiddle.

Swift brought a voice to country music that had seldom been heard in the genre: the voice of a young woman. Traditionally, female performers in country have adopted the stance of an older, experienced woman toughened by hard living and romantic betrayal. Swift, by contrast, presented herself as a teenager reporting on her life as she experienced it. She

sings of the urgency of young love ("Our Song"), of yearning for someone who's unavailable ("You Belong with Me"), of feeling socially isolated ("The Outside"), and of navigating life's transitions ("Fifteen"). By expressing directly how it feels to be young—both the euphoria and the heartbreak— she garnered the fierce loyalty of a self-organized online community of young fans who call themselves Swifties, many of whom feel that they have grown up alongside her.

Swift left her mark on country music. In the wake of her huge success, the Nashville industry establishment became more

open to cultivating young performers. Whereas it has long been standard in country music for singers to record songs written for them by professional songwriters, Swift helped to open the door to singer-songwriters in the genre. Her self-conscious transition from country to pop was accompanied by a transition to a more adult outlook. Gone are the fiddles and Dobros, replaced largely by a rock sound, electronics, and dance beats, making her work less warm but edgier. Gone also is Swift's dewy-eyed romantic perspective, replaced by a harder-edged, more aggressive attitude. Whereas some of Swift's country songs are first-person narratives and some are in the third person, her work becomes intensely personal, charting her move to New York City and her life as a celebrity whose every move is fodder for the paparazzi and tabloids. She depicts romantic relationships as zero-sum games and uses her songs to take righteous revenge on former lovers.

"If they don't like you for being yourself, be yourself even more."

—Taylor Swift

212 Taylor Swift onstage in Rutherford, New Jersey, during her 1989 World Tour in 2015.

212–213 Taylor Swift performs at the iHeart Music Festival in Las Vegas, 2014.

Although Swift argues that her image as a "player" and "serial dater" (her words) is a media fabrication, she knowingly plays into and exploits it, particularly in the song "Blank Space," one of her biggest hits.

In 2020, during the COVID pandemic, Swift recorded two quiet and reflective albums, *Folklore* and *Evermore*, whose style is closer to that of folk ballads with some elements of country than to her high-gloss pop. These albums return Swift to the small-town setting of her earliest songs, no longer seen from the perspective of an exuberant teenager trying to find her way but from that of a mature observer taking stock. Whereas "Our Song" reveled in the excitement of a secretive relationship conducted behind the backs of parents, "Illicit Affairs" tallies up the psychic damage of trying to maintain a clandestine tryst. Whereas the music video for the earlier song shows a cheerful Swift sitting on the front porch in a Southern belle dress or lounging in a sea of rose petals, the video for the later one is a static, twilit image of an empty road.

SOUTHERN CALIFORNIA SUNSHINE

THE BANGLES

> The Bangles' classic lineup. From left: Vicki Peterson, Susanna Hoffs, Debbi Peterson, and Michael "Micki" Steele.

In the early 1980s, a collection of young musicians based in Los Angeles who shared what Bangles guitarist Vicki Peterson calls "our fierce love of the music of the 60s" came to be known as the Paisley Underground, a reference to a fashion trend of the earlier era. Each of the groups on this scene identified with a specific band from the sixties. The all-women group the Bangles took the Beatles as their inspiration. Like their Merseyside predecessors, all of the Bangles write songs, play, and sing, sharing lead vocals. Their approach to vocal harmony,

which is a keystone of their sound, reflects the influence of both the Beatles and Southern Californian groups of the 1960s, particularly the Mamas and the Papas.

The Bangles got started in 1980 when singer and guitarist Susanna Hoffs, inspired by the successful all-female group the Go-Gos, set out in search of other women with whom to form a band. This quest led her to sisters Vicki and Debbi Peterson, the latter a drummer, who had been working together in several groups. Discovering common ground in their passion for the Beatles and 60s

garage rock, the three began performing together regularly in clubs around Los Angeles, joined by bassist Annette Zilinskas. Perhaps inspired by the famous Beatle haircut, they first recorded as the Bangs, but they were forced to change their name just before releasing their recordings when another group that was already using it threatened to sue.

The early Bangles, which Hoffs has described as a "scrappy band," attracted the attention of Columbia Records, leading to their first album, *All Over the Place*, in 1984. Zilinskas left the group

just before the album was recorded, and Michael "Micki" Steele, who had worked with Joan Jett in the first iteration of the Runaways, joined on bass and vocals. Their second album, *Different Light* (1986), catapulted the band to international fame on the strength of the singles "Manic Monday," which peaked at #2 in the United States, the United Kingdom, and Germany, and "Walk Like an Egyptian," #2 in the United Kingdom and #1 in the United States. They would have one more global #1 hit with "Eternal Flame" from their third album, *Everything* (1988).

By any measure, the Bangles were one of the most successful female rock bands of all time.

Over the course of these three albums, the Bangles' recorded sound became progressively more polished and elaborately produced, moving further and further from their garage roots. They remained much scrappier in concert, thanks to Vicki Peterson's aggressive lead guitar and Hoffs's folky rhythm guitar, anchored by Debbi Peterson's muscular drumming and Steele's thunderous but agile bass lines. Although they stuck largely to tightly composed pop songs, their performances of

them veered closer to hard rock. The Bangles felt increasingly as if they were being held captive in what Steele describes as "this sort of hit machine" and losing their creative autonomy as musicians. Exhausted from seven years of relentless touring, the Bangles disbanded in 1989. Hoffs pursued a solo career, the Petersons worked with other groups, and Steele withdrew from the music industry.

By 1999, the Bangles had found their way back to each other and regrouped. Refusing to be characterized as an eighties nostalgia act, they recorded two well-received

albums of new material, *Doll Revolution* (2003) and *Sweetheart of the Sun* (2011), the latter a tribute to the Laurel Canyon folk-rock scene of the 1960s. Steele left the group in 2005 and was eventually replaced by original bassist Annette Zilinskas.

The Bangles continue to perform concerts, often sharing the bill with other women musicians. Coming full circle, in 2019, they participated in *3 x 4*, a recording project for which they and three other re-united bands from the Paisley Underground performed songs by each of the other three groups.

QUEEN OF
ROCK AND ROLL
TINA TURNER

Tina Turner has been inducted into the Rock and Roll Hall of Fame twice: as half of the duo Ike and Tina Turner and as a solo artist. Turner, born Anna Mae Bullock in Tennessee, had moved with her mother to St. Louis as a teenager and took part in the burgeoning rhythm and blues scene there. She joined Ike Turner and His Kings of Rhythm in 1957 as a featured singer; by 1960 she was the focal presence in the Ike and Tina Turner Revue. In 1976, she extricated herself from an increasingly abusive relationship with Ike Turner, leaving with nothing and painstakingly rebuilding her career. She finally burst through in 1984 with her

album *Private Dancer* and the #1 pop single "What's Love Got to Do With It." Since retiring from performing in 2007, the only recordings Turner has made pertain to her Buddhist faith. In May 2023, Tina Turner died in Switzerland after a long illness.

In the 1960s, the Ike and Tina Turner Revue developed a reputation for electrifying live performances. The revue was a well-oiled machine with many moving parts and included Ike Turner's tight, horn-driven band and a three-woman girl group called the Ikettes, and featured male vocalists in addition to Tina Turner. By the mid-1960s, the show was structured so

218 Photo of Tina Turner in 1964 at the time of the Ike and Tina Turner Revue.

219 Proof sheet of Tina Turner posing for a photo, 1964.

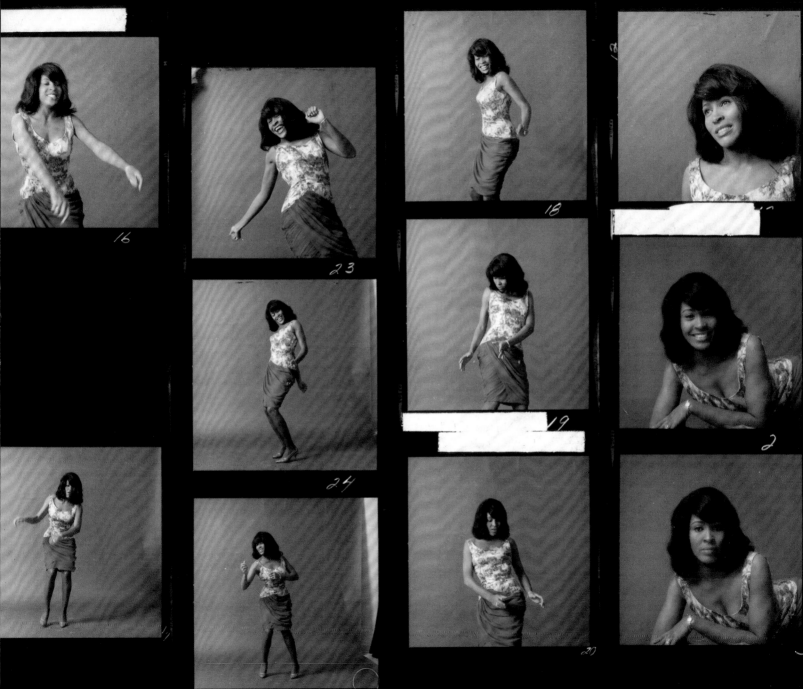

220 Ike and Tina Turner and the Ikettes in 1968. From left to right: Ann Thomas, Paulette Parker, Ike Turner (rear), Tina Turner (front), Pat Powdrill, and Jean Brown.

221 Tina Turner (standing left) and Ike Turner (seated) on the French television Christmas special *Poiret Est à Vous (Poiret Is Yours)* hosted by the actor Jean Poiret in 1975.

all the other parts led up to Tina Turner's appearances, with the Ikettes as her backup singers. She brought intense energy and a commanding presence to the stage as she danced along with the Ikettes, gyrated around the stage, and belted out rhythm and blues in a powerful, rough-hewn voice that alternated a soaring gospel sound with down-to-earth bluesiness. This voice was a formidable instrument that it took Turner some time to master. On "You're Just a Fool in Love" (1960), she brings life to a rhythm and blues song with a funky groove, but unleashes her voice from the beginning, leaving no room for development. By "It's Gonna Work Out Fine" (1961), she has begun to assert control, building from a smooth texture into a raspy gospel shout. The Ike and Tina Turner Revue did not perform many original songs—the group focused on crowd-pleasing, high-energy presentations of the soul hits of the day, moving more toward funk in the 1970s. Along the way, however, Tina Turner emerged as a songwriter. "Nutbush City Limits," a hit in 1973, is her portrait of a small rural town like the one where she spent her early childhood.

222 Tina Turner performing in The Hague, 1982.

223 Tina Turner performing in 1975 as part of the Ike and Tina Turner Revue.

224 Tina Turner performing at Wembley Arena in London during the *Break Every Rule* tour in 1987.

225 Tina Turner during a concert held at Hammersmith Odeon in London in 1982.

In 1985, Turner embarked on the first of many record-breaking tours as a solo artist; by 2000, she was the highest-earning touring popular musician in the world. In concert, Turner retained the fire and intensity of her earlier incarnation but presented herself like a rock artist, fronting a band using rock instrumentation. Her concerts became more elaborate, involving backup singers with whom she danced as she had with the Ikettes, costume changes, and more varied staging. During the song "Private Dancer," about a stripper or prostitute, Turner sang sitting down while her female dancers, also on chairs, wore corsets and heavy makeup and kicked up their legs, illustrating the song's subject matter. While these styles of performing distinguished Tina Turner the solo artist from Tina Turner of the revue, she brought these two identities together on her Twenty Four Seven tour of 2000, in which Turner promised to take the audience "on the journey of my career this evening, starting from now all the way back to the beginning." The first step on this journey was a performance of "You're Just a Fool in Love" with her backup singers staged as a girl group and black-and-white footage of Turner performing with the Ikettes in the early 1960s projected on giant video screens.

SISTERS IN ARMS

ANN and NANCY WILSON

< Ann and Nancy Wilson
in Hollywood in 1976 at
the time of the release
of Heart's first album,
Dreamboat Annie.

< Ann and Nancy Wilson
in Hollywood in 1976 at
the time of the release
of Heart's first album,
Dreamboat Annie.

In 1977, Ann Wilson, who with her sister Nancy Wilson is the creative nucleus of the hard rock band Heart, told an interviewer, "I hate being asked what it's like to be a woman in the rock business." Although the Wilsons prefer to be thought of as musicians plain and simple, they do not hesitate to speak out against the sexism they have encountered in their career. In the same interview, Ann Wilson described the song "White Lightning & Wine" from their first album, *Dreamboat Annie* (1975), as an angry diatribe against rock musicians who take sexual advantage of young women, written from the predator's perspective. When performing the song, she portrays the protagonist as a malevolent figure; her characteristic upward leaps in vocal register on certain words make him seem even more menacing. The Wilsons wrote "Barracuda" (1977), one of Heart's best-known songs, in response to their record label's idea of constructing a publicity campaign implying that the two sisters were lovers. Incensed, they composed an indictment of industry types who try "to fit you into a very small box as a woman with sexuality and objectification," in the words of Nancy Wilson. The close connection between the Wilsons'

227

228 Nancy Wilson, playing acoustic guitar, and Ann Wilson, playing electric guitar, perform with Heart at the Portland Memorial Coliseum in 1977.

life experiences and their songs is also evident from "Magic Man" (1975), about a young woman's infatuation with an older, seductive man. With the passing of time, Ann Wilson has often chosen not to perform the song, as the experience to which it refers becomes more distant.

Ann and Nancy Wilson grew up in Seattle and began their musical careers as young adults, at first separately. Nancy, a guitarist and singer, became a folk musician. In 1970, Ann, a singer and multi-instrumentalist, linked up with Heart, a rock band based in Vancouver that had existed in various forms since 1963. Nancy joined her sister in the band in 1974. Although Ann is the primary lead singer known for her powerful belting voice, wide range, and precise control, Nancy sang lead on the group's first #1 hit, "These Dreams," in 1986, and the sisters are recognized for the tightness of their harmonies. After developing an audience and garnering respectable sales of *Dreamboat Annie*, Heart entered the US market on the strength of "Magic Man," a Top 10 hit. They toured extensively, playing large venues. Although Nancy found the transition from the acoustic guitar she played as a folk musician to an electric guitar to be difficult, she became the group's sole lead guitarist in 1979 and is widely recognized as a superlative rock guitarist.

229 Heart performing at the Oakland Coliseum in 1977. From left to right: Roger Fisher (guitar), Nancy Wilson (guitar), Ann Wilson (vocals), Howard Leese (guitar), and Steve Fossen (bass guitar). Not pictured: Mike Derosier (drums).

The Wilson sisters profess to being great admirers of Led Zeppelin, and aspects of Heart's sound reflect this influence. Heart combines acoustic and electric instrumentation in songs that often juxtapose folk and hard rock styles, an approach that entails a sophisticated manipulation of dynamics. "Crazy on You" (1975) is a case in point. The song opens with Nancy's folky finger-picked acoustic guitar solo, which becomes a strummed rhythm guitar figure. The rock band kicks in at that point, with an initially restrained vocal performance by Ann that builds until she unleashes her full power on the chorus after the song's bridge.

After a strong showing in the second half of the 1970s, Heart experienced diminished success, but the band rebounded in the mid-1980s with two more songs at #1 and three popular albums. From 1991 until 1997, the Wilsons owned a recording studio called Bad Animals, the title of one of their albums, where many of the key figures of Seattle grunge made their records. The Wilson sisters became doyennes of the Seattle music scene, offering personal and professional support to a younger generation of musicians.

CHANTEUSE

AMY WINEHOUSE

Amy Winehouse's hit "Rehab" (2006) was simultaneously retro and immediate. It could have been a lost Motown record, except that its depiction of an unrepentant addict's refusal to undergo treatment was a topic Motown would never have touched. Winehouse's performance persona enshrined a similar paradox. Her beehive hairstyle, thick eyeliner, and the slinky gowns or cocktail dresses she wore evoked a bygone era of smoky nightclubs. The horn-laden jazz and soul stylings of her band, along with her strong alto voice and assertive delivery, also seemed to belong to another time and place. Her songs, on the other hand, were direct, personal,

and confessional in a manner that was distinctly contemporary, more akin to the singer-songwriters of the 1970s than to her blues and soul forebearers of the 1950s and 1960s. "Rehab," for one, derived from an episode in which Winehouse's management tried to persuade her to be treated for substance abuse. Her defiant response, reflected in the song's references to Ray Charles and Donny Hathaway, was to insist on the curative power of music: "People that go into rehabilitation don't have music in their lives."

Winehouse grew up in a suburban London household where big band and modern jazz records were continually on the

turntable. Her own early musical interests leaned toward R&B and hip-hop. She put together a rap group, Sweet 'N' Sour, modeled on Salt-N-Peppa, when she was ten years old. After surreptitiously playing her brother's electric guitar, she acquired her own guitar around the age of thirteen and began writing songs. Winehouse's first album, *Frank* (2003), is a jazz record that opens with Winehouse's scat singing. Winehouse's vocal style is distinctive. She alternates staccato emphasis of certain words with legato passages, extending words by adding extra syllables. Her sometimes-slurred delivery flows over bar lines as she sings

> Amy Winehouse performs at the Isle of Wight Festival in 2007.

232 Amy Winehouse poses backstage at the Jazz Cafe in Camden, London, 2004.

233 Amy Winehouse in Rotterdam, Netherlands, 2004.

both with and against the beat. It was on her second album, *Back to Black* (2006), that Winehouse refined her style. She moved away from jazz to forge a sound from elements of classic R&B and soul, Motown, the girl groups of the 1960s, and female pop singers of the same era. Her singing emphasizes her lower register and is more carefully calibrated than on the earlier album. The narratives of Winehouse's songs are typically set in the hotel rooms, bars, and apartments where secretive, sometimes anonymous, usually adulterous, liaisons take place. Winehouse's posture on both albums is that of a world-weary observer. The dominant emotion of the typical Winehouse protagonist in songs such as "He Can Only Hold Her" and "Stronger Than Me" is disillusionment with the vacant women and weak men she sees around her. Songs in the vein of "You Know That I'm No Good" and "Back to Black" convey this protagonist's disappointment in herself. Her attempts to be faithful and sober are continuously undermined by desire and all too readily available opportunities to fulfill it. Because these trysts are inevitably unsatisfying, she ends up seeking the solace of alcohol. The Scottish singer KT Tunstall describes Winehouse's affect well: "I don't think you get a voice like that for free. You have to go through some hard experiences to sing what she sings about and sing the way she does."

In her all too brief career, Winehouse produced only these two albums. A third, posthumous album, *Lioness: Hidden Treasures* (2011), provided further evidence of Winehouse's embrace of the girl-group sound and popular music of the 1960s. She succumbed to her addictions and passed away in 2011 at the age of twenty-seven, leaving behind a small but indelible body of work.

234 Amy Winehouse at the Highline
Ballroom in New York City during her 2007
Back to Black tour.

235 Amy Winehouse, c. 2007.

236 Amy Winehouse sings at the
Glastonbury Festival, 2006.

"Every bad situation is a blues song
waiting to happen."

ABOUT THE AUTHOR

PHILIP AUSLANDER is a professor of performance studies and popular musicology in the School of Literature, Media, and Communication at the Georgia Institute of Technology (Atlanta, Georgia, US). He writes on music, performance, and visual art, and is the author of numerous articles and seven books, including *Performing Glam Rock: Gender and Theatricality in Popular Music*, *In Concert: Performing Musical Persona*, and three editions of *Liveness: Performance in a Mediatized Culture*. *Dr. Blues*, a short film Auslander wrote, produced, and acted in, premiered at the Peachtree Village International Film Festival in Atlanta in 2019.

The author wishes to thank Giorgio Ferrero, Rebecca Fishman, Sean Klappenbach, Karina Teichert, and the woman who rocks his world, Deanna Sirlin.

PHOTO CREDITS

Editorial Project

Valeria Manferto De Fabianis

Editorial Assistant

Giorgio Ferrero

Graphic Layout

Paola Piacco

whitestar°

WS whitestar™ is a trademark of White Star s.r.l.

© 2023 White Star s.r.l.
Piazzale Luigi Cadorna, 6
20123 Milan, Italy
www.whitestar.it

Editing: Abby Young

ISBN 978-88-544-2035-9
2 3 4 5 6 28 27 6 25 24

Printed in China

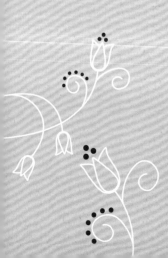